What people are saying about …

CALLING

"Brantley's book provides a strong foundation for anyone searching for meaning in work. He challenges readers to be free of lesser purposes while pointing them toward honor, purpose, and altruism. Readers will appreciate Brantley's clear and literary writing style, strong faith-based teaching, and honest and helpful personal examples of finding success in a career. This is a book to study, learn from, and enjoy."

Marcus Brotherton, *New York Times* bestselling author

"Many of us are going through life wondering if there is something better, missing out on the purpose God has for us right where we are, and right where we are headed. *Calling: Awaken to the Purpose of Your Work* by Pierce Brantley offers us a changed perspective on what it means to have a called career."

Jonathan McKee, author

CALLING

CALLING

AWAKEN TO THE
PURPOSE OF
YOUR WORK

PIERCE
BRANTLEY

DAVID C COOK

transforming lives together

CALLING
Published by David C Cook
4050 Lee Vance Drive
Colorado Springs, CO 80918 U.S.A.

Integrity Music Limited, a Division of David C Cook
Brighton, East Sussex BN1 2RE, England

The graphic circle C logo is a registered trademark of David C Cook.

The website addresses recommended throughout this book are offered as a
resource to you. These websites are not intended in any way to be or imply an
endorsement on the part of David C Cook, nor do we vouch for their content.

Details in some stories have been changed to protect the identities of the persons involved.

Library of Congress Control Number 2019948091
ISBN 978-0-8307-8073-0
eISBN 978-0-8307-8076-1

© 2020 Pierce Brantley

The Team: Michael Covington, Jeff Gerke, Megan Stengel,
Kayla Fenstermaker, Jon Middel, Susan Murdock
Cover Design: Nick Lee
Cover Photo: Getty Images

Printed in the United States of America
First Edition 2020

1 2 3 4 5 6 7 8 9 10

031019

For Tim, my father.
Thank you for your example,
consistency, and spirit.

CONTENTS

ACKNOWLEDGMENTS

This book, like everything in my life, is an outcome of Christ's unshaking love in my life. I am so grateful for Jesus' original work that made this book and my new life in him possible. To my wife, Kristie, thank you for standing by me, making me coffee, and letting me mull over the meanings of words out loud. You're a trooper and I love you. To Nick, thank you for taking a chance on me, answering endless questions, and for your wisdom. I'm so grateful. To Michael and my tribe at Cook, you're incredibly talented. I've loved working with you. To Joe, thank you for your friendship and for encouraging me to write the book to begin with. You play a part in this. Mark, thank you for teaching me to live in reality. God bless you. To my mother: thank you for baseboards, baskets of laundry, and for bringing me books at an early age.

INTRODUCTION

Work. Our jobs. What we do to pay the bills. It's part of life.

But there's a secret to work that most Christian men haven't discovered. Paul knew this secret. Elijah and David too. But most men never discover it. Many can identify the itch, but they simply can't scratch it.

The itch troubles you like a gentle prod, a niggling little thought that the work you do during the day isn't everything it's meant to be. You feel as if you're missing something when you clock in and clock out. Your work doesn't get the job done spiritually, you could say. Nor is it very fulfilling.

That's the itch, and it can lead to a great discovery. But it's also really easy to dismiss.

So men continue to endure the daily grind, missing out on the faith and secret strength that could overflow in their work. This results in whole generations of Christian men who work hard but don't know why. Or—worse—who never learn the real work they are called to do.

Which is a tragedy. There is so much at stake—and so little time to stake a claim on a calling.

There is hope, however, for the man who wants to know what God might give him to do with the few days he has. So long as you haven't stopped working, it's never too late to find the purpose of your work.

It's no mistake that you're reading this book now. If it's in your hands, a new work life is around the corner for you.

Our ancient fathers of the faith knew the secret of meaningful work. They knew what was required of them. They could see the purpose in their work a mile away. This faith gave them a life of biblical proportions. In part, because they knew how to focus their energy. They knew the work they were meant to do. This assurance gave them all the courage and foresight they needed during the day. It helped men like Moses, Daniel, and Joseph be diligent in everyday jobs and participate in more eternal outcomes than the average Joe.

The secret can be yours as well. The principles of work they employed, described in this book, are available to you. My prayer, brother, is that you learn them, love them, and use them to partner with the Almighty in incredible new ways.

You will discover the special and specific work God has for you. Best of all, you can move into your calling at any job, with any boss, at any place in life as well.

We're talking about *vocation* here, which is based on the Latin word *vocare*, meaning "to call or summon." Whether you're aware of the calling in your vocation or not, God is *calling* you to it.

God hasn't passed you by. He has a race for you to run—and that's true even if you feel disconnected from the race. Neither is God upset by your circumstances. Just because you might feel hopeless now or unsure about the future, it does not mean that the Almighty doesn't have a great work life for you.

He is *for* you, after all.

So take courage: you are about to learn how to work in and through your calling, which you will find within the working day. You'll receive the benefit of laboring alongside the Lord and the special blessing that can be for a man such as yourself. This blessing is a life rich in stories of partnering with God, seeing his kingdom advance, and knowing, for certain, that you're living out your calling. If you ask me, there is no other way to live.

There is no end to God's kingdom, no shortage of his strength. God has a massive treasury of power and goodness, and he draws freely from that supernatural bank account to support his sons and daughters. These riches are meant for more than Sunday mornings or a few mountaintop moments over a lifetime. The goodness of God has practical nine-to-five implications for every man who wants to know what it looks like to live in partnership with the Lord.

And no, you don't need to become a pastor, worship leader, or minister to get access to this supernatural bank account. The agency of the Almighty extends to any man who wants the joy of gainful employment with the Lord.

As you'll learn in *Calling*, there are no collar colors in Christ. Only men who work with the Lord and those who don't. The men who don't can only wish for great stories. The men who do actually have them.

You're the latter, of course, which is why you're here.

While it would be nice to have a vocation whose spiritual value is obvious, like being a preacher or working for a ministry, most Christian men end up having to just get a job.

They think it should be possible to integrate their faith and their profession, but they don't know how. They feel a vague sense of duty but never feel passionate about their job. They clock in and clock out, all the while wondering, *Is this all there is?*

What if it didn't have to be that way?

What if you could find your calling within your career? What if you could find meaning in what you're already doing? What if all you need is a change of perspective on what it means to have a called career?

Calling guides you toward that fulfilling career. You want to connect with God in your work in a meaningful way. You were designed for this partnership, and it's how you will find real purpose. You do have a calling in your career, and this book will help you find it.

Right.

Let's get to work.

Chapter 1

THE SPIRIT AND
THE SPATULA

I praise you, for I am fearfully and wonderfully made.
Wonderful are your works; my soul knows it very well.

—Psalm 139:14

You know how people say, "Hey, shut the door—were you raised in a barn?"

Well, I really was raised in a barn. (But I do shut the door after myself. Usually.)

I grew up in the East Texas piney woods. Literally in a barn. The living situation was supposed to be only temporary, of course. We thought we'd live in the barn on the property until our family's ship came in and then our house would quickly be built. For seventeen years we waited on Providence to provide, but that ship never did come in.

Houses, I learned, rarely build themselves.

That barn was completely exposed to the elements. The summers were sweltering, and it wasn't uncommon for a snake to be found in a shaded corner of a room. One summer a hive of bees paused their migration and spent three days in the rafters. Winters, conversely, were colder than your fridge.

One of my first jobs was mowing. That always struck me as odd. At first I thought mowing the grass around the barn would keep the grasshoppers out of our living areas. But it didn't. I mean, the barn was surrounded by acres of knee-high grass, and cutting the grass didn't keep the critters out. In fact, many of them would jump toward the barn to avoid the blade. But what else does one do with so much grass and time?

In those early years, as I worked our fifteen-acre yard, something surprising happened: a bond grew between me and the Lord. As I mowed, I worshipped and I listened. And God met me in my work.

A relationship grew out of a seemingly pointless task, and that made all the difference in what I was doing. It might be hard to believe about a young boy and yard work, but I actually began to look forward to cutting paths in the wilderness. To spending that work time with God. It was an exodus for an East Texas boy.

Years later, after I left that wilderness and had some business success, the Lord met me again in a profound way. He showed me a vision. It was as if I looked up and saw a wide television in the air. In the vision he revealed he had a plan for the house of which our family had dreamed. His idea of home and happiness had never changed.

As the vision unfolded, I was taken from Southlake, Texas, back to the old slab where our country home should have been. The grass was uncut, and everything looked elemental.

Suddenly a man appeared with a huge hammer. He walked up and held his hand out toward me. "Give me the plans and I will build the house." The man was stoic and resolved, ready for action and my answer. But in the vision I couldn't speak. "Give me the plans," he repeated, "and I will build the house."

In a blink the vision ended, and I was back in Southlake.

The point was simple: God wanted to complete the good work he had started, to build on a foundation that was already laid. But this good work would require real stewardship, not simply doing work for its own sake.

His promise was to do the building, but I had to begin the work myself.

So let's get to work.

A CALLED CAREER

Faithful Christian men long for a calling. We wish we could join God in his works. We itch for a great reason to get out of bed in the morning and head out into the world to accomplish meaningful things.

But … the rent's due. So, rather than waiting for the perfect job to come along or for their ship to come in, Christian men put on their boots and go out to just earn a paycheck.

This is difficult for most Christian men. We serve a mighty, universal God whose plans involve the whole world, and we long to be part of those plans. We do what we can at church and such, but we struggle to find purpose at work, and we don't know why. We mean well, and we work hard, but a piece of the puzzle always seems to be missing.

A steady job—at a desk or work site—fixes the immediate problem of income, but it may come at the cost of a man's longing for meaningful work.

If something feels off in your work life, that's because it is. Your spirit hums to a different rhythm from the world's rhythm—which is why your faith doesn't always feel functional and why it may feel like a cog that doesn't fit the machine.

I'd like to suggest something that you may not have heard before, but I think you'll get it as soon as you read it: work is the connective tissue that binds your career and Christlikeness.

When you work with Christ, your inner man is strengthened. You are joined to God's higher purposes. And you inherit what I have termed a called career: a deep, tangible, overflowing life of specific work for the kingdom and set apart for one man—you.

Sound good? Sound like what you're longing for? I get it.

But though this is a gift offered to all Christian men, it's a gift that usually stays wrapped. Hidden and waiting for us to enjoy in our hereafter home.

On the other hand, some men work diligently every day to find purpose in their work, to have a job that provides that connective tissue, but they never find the right fit. When this goes on for a prolonged time, it creates a form of atrophy. It breaks down the practical, Spirit-filled connection your day could have. And this, in turn, robs you of the vision and energy the Almighty has provided. In effect, you lose strength. You settle. Maybe you've experienced this.

Meaningful work means *working well*. But what does that look like? It's not just working harder. It's not pulling all-nighters or earning higher pay or getting promoted. It's not even finding the right job or organization to work for. An employee at McDonald's who understands the secret of a called career can be more fulfilled by what he does than a pastor of a megachurch.

God has a specific job plan for you personally.

The key is learning how to step into his work environment.

NEW SHOES

The best I could do was a Sharpie marker.

It wasn't shoe polish, but it would get the job done. Besides, you could really tell the difference only when the sun shone on them directly. I had reglued the soles of my other shoes a handful of times, and they still kept falling apart. The separating backs made an obnoxious clapping sound as I walked and would introduce me anywhere I went. So, old as they were, these shoes and their Sharpie-spotted polish would have to do for the time being.

Perfect or not, I had places to go.

For a kid of thirteen, this felt like a lot of resolve. My circumstances were not going to dictate my actions, even if I had been raised in a barn. I was going to control the situation as best I could. The personal pride was genuine too—it was as if my ability to mend my shoes translated into the power to keep life knit up as well.

Our work lives can feel like that. Work is forward momentum in the face of uncertainty. We step boldly into it, even if the work itself is not exactly what we'd like it to be. We can imagine a better future, sure. We might even believe God himself has a better idea in mind. But how do we find it? Maybe it's best just to keep walking forward, hoping things will get better.

After all, a little bit of spit shine will go a long way to polish your outlook.

The truth is, we can't just will ourselves into having meaningful work. We can't fault a guy for wanting to change his stars, but the reality is that a man's *resolve* and his *righteousness* are not the same things. You are set apart for good works from the Lord—it's true. But you can't white-knuckle yourself into them. All that does is put Sharpie on reglued shoes. Only God's resolve will transform a circumstance into a calling.

He alone will give you new shoes to walk in.

CLAY IN THE POTTER'S HANDS

Most Christian men who long for purpose in their work lives start by praying for Sunday to spill over into Monday. Our hope is that we'll be able to splash a little sanctification from our time at church onto those around us at the workplace. For many men, this lasts only until things need to get done. Then it's back to business as usual. Whatever he got from Sunday morning is helpful all the way until crunch time, when he may find himself trading in the pew for pragmatism.

Praise God that our stories don't have to end there.

Here's what's possible for your work: you will be clay in the holy Potter's hand; you will know that everything you commit your hands to will involve his divine craftsmanship. You will come to the place where you're not pushing yourself to go to work but where the work itself will be propelling you. You will see that the vessel you want to be is exactly the vessel you are being molded into.

If that sounds good to you, the question you must ask yourself is this: "Am I engaged in the process of being molded?"

Knowing the answer removes every condemning thought and doubtful question. *Is this the right job? Did I make a wrong turn in life? Is there a reason so-and-so is more successful?* A man given to the Lord *will* be used for a higher purpose because he's being made into his Maker's desired image. You are uniquely made for the task at hand.

We have to understand that work is not a job—it is an attitude toward a job. Hopelessness comes when you confuse the two.

There are no dead-end jobs in Christ.

We need to have our minds renewed by Christ until we can see this. When this happens, we see meaning grow from the mundane. We find joy in a job description. Our calling isn't the work itself but is the kingdom purpose in it. God has a specific assignment for you in whatever it is you do as your job—a mission within your work.

Now, walking in this reality does not come naturally for most of us. We rarely see purpose in our jobs, and by 10:00 a.m. on Monday, any sense of purpose is pushed out by the demands of the job. So how do we participate in the practical work of sanctification, the hour-by-hour transformation that occurs during the working day?

We must start with the foundation, the role that labor has in our lives. This is the key to fulfillment in what you do.

Let's stop here for a moment. If you feel disillusioned, don't worry. For many of us, the wrong idea we have about work started with the way we grew up. Everything around us says to measure who we are and the success of what we do by the accolades we receive or the connections we have.

But there are empty men with many accolades and full men with none. Fulfillment has little to do with trophy rooms.

Think of your labor as a holy container. Your work is a vessel full of love, whose sole purpose is to be poured out as an offering back to almighty God. The way you work is your response to God for giving you work in the first place. The more you respond to God in love, the more meaningful your work will become.

If you feel an emptiness or lack of meaning in your work, consider whether you see your labor as a love offering to God.

Do you want evidence that your work has become worshipful? Then pause to assess what meaning you presently receive from your work. This is your barometer.

You were designed to increase in good work. Your sacrifice and your success, spiritually speaking, are intimately tied together. Part of why I wrote *Calling* is to show that the less you pour out, the emptier you'll feel. The more you give, the more you'll receive.

You'll bring new power into your day when you live from this kingdom dynamic. The principles that govern your calling and the work connected to it will be unlocked. The unique blend of anointing and Spirit-infused talent the Lord has given you will be unleashed as well. In fact, if you learn to labor in this special type of love, to work out your salvation in your work, you will bring a new measure of abundance into both your life and your career.

Jesus said, "I came that they may have life and have it abundantly" (John 10:10).

Put another way, he came to break the nine-to-five.

SHIPS AND STEWARDSHIP

Every man, if he's honest, has wondered whether work can be fulfilling. He may have "just a job," and that can make the question "What do you do?" feel like an interrogation. *Do I justify, lie, or change the subject?* Doubt that work can be fulfilling can create a mental tug-of-war, a lingering angst that your ship may have sailed without you. Add the realization that others have reached levels of success that you have not reached, and this fear can make you catatonic.

We can rest in prayer, taking all our anxieties to Christ and knowing that he has our good in mind. But sometimes we can still worry.

Part of us wants to quit and go looking for a job with more meaning. But who knows what could happen if we gave up on this job, which we know, to look for fulfillment in a new job we don't know?

Don't rock the boat, the mind says. *There is more to be lost than gained.* Twenty years later, the boat has never been rocked, but it hasn't gone anywhere either. It's a sad reality for many men. Your flesh will give you endless reasons to reject vision as well. Fears and insecurities and even certain pleasures (or the avoidance of pain) can give you a million reasons to never raise your sails. If you listen to them, years will slip away in silence.

Maybe you feel you were born into the wrong family, have a poor education, or experienced some tragedy that prevents you from having the work life you wish you could have. My friend, you may have been victimized by many terrible things, but only you can turn yourself into a permanent victim. Don't do it.

Perhaps life just got busy. Being too busy—filling all your time with stuff, even good stuff—is a way many Christian men agree with their flesh. The agreement leaves you empty. Endorphin-driven exhaustion.

Still others feel they have legitimate reasons for never taking action to get a called career. If this is you, ask the Holy Spirit whether you're making decisions out of fear or facts. He'll tell you. He can also change the facts.

When we look through the lens of heaven's power, no reason or excuse is revealed to be legitimate. With God, there is always the promise of a new beginning. You have a Christ-backed guarantee for your future. If you choose not to abide in this reality—and it is a choice—you're like a would-be sailor who enjoys the pier more than the sea.

The Almighty wants to give you a new vision for the working day, but you have to let him. Today could be the day it all turns around for you at work. God doesn't despise small beginnings (see Zech. 4:10 NLT), and neither should we.

Your vocation is one of the main centers where God wants to do his work. He put you in that job on purpose. He put you in that department on purpose. He put you on that crew, next to that one guy or with that one chief, by design. Strategically. Imagine if God had complete control of you in that place of work. Imagine if he had total access to speak and work through you on the job. Just picture that for a minute.

That's where we're going.

TALENTS AND TIME

Make no mistake: the Enemy will try to lull you into wishful thinking. He doesn't want you presenting your members to Christ (see Rom. 6:13)! He wants you thinking and whining about how fulfilling work is never given to you. My friend, this is the emotional equivalent of burying your talent.

If you are familiar with Jesus' parable of the talents (see Matt. 25:14–30), you may remember that a rich man entrusted varying amounts of money to several of his servants. His focus was on whether each man would display faithful stewardship of what he'd been given.

Upon his return, he learned that two of the servants had displayed good stewardship and one had not. His anger at the lazy servant had nothing to do with the amount of money he had been given to work with. His frustration was with the man's attitude. He knew the man could've done well with what he had, yet he chose not to (he buried the money and then dug it up and gave it back to the rich man), at least partially out of fear. Which is profound.

In a sense, the man's pocket was already full of the Lord's provision. What did he have to fear?

How high is the Lord's ceiling? How much increase can he cause? Have you tested it? God is not cruel. Nor is he unaware of your circumstances. He knows that buried talents do not produce dividends—not for you, not for him, and not for those you could bless.

Fulfilling work starts here: by recognizing what has been placed in your hands to steward and then by wisely investing it back in the world for the good of the kingdom.

What has been placed in your hands? Have you asked him? Maybe you think you've been shortchanged when it comes to talent, opportunity, money, or time. God hasn't shortchanged anyone. We each, equally, can choose gratitude for what we have. Anyway, even if you are "less blessed" than someone else, is that really an excuse to not use your talent? Is any of this really a problem for God? Five loaves can feed five thousand (see Matt. 14:15–21).

Your pocket is already filled with the Lord's provision too. You can do things other people can't. You know things other people don't. You have physical or mental capabilities other people don't. You have advantages other people don't. Go on—take a look at what's in your pocket. Make a list of your skills, opportunities, attributes, and gifts.

Your job is a vital part of your entire life. You don't have your work life over here and your spiritual life over there. We're all mixed all the time. Lean into this. Be faithfully aware that the minutes of the workday are the actual, specific parts of your Christian life. They are when your spiritual life happens. Your work is holy, even if your job is not.

Satan, however, would like to convince us otherwise. He'd love for us to consider our work meaningless. He'd prefer us to leave church at church and not try to bring it to work. But God permeates our existence. Can you really call anything busywork when you are filled with favor from on high?

The Lord has set every man's feet on two parallel paths: one spiritual and one earthly. We exist in both realms for now. The task of the Christian is to live on the earth in a spiritual way. To always be mindful of the Spirit even as we attend to the tasks of the earth.

When we do that, we experience natural advancement along the path of promotion. A Spirit-led worker is naturally going to do the things that make for good and honest service to his coworkers, clients, bosses, and company. And this will lead to promotions, though promotions were not the primary goal.

The problems come when we try to lead with the wrong foot. Earthly goals and earthly means will often result in fleshly outcomes. This means we must train our hearts to care about the details of what we do and to see them as part of our stewardship. This is the daily, practical process of denying our flesh.

What cannot be redeemed? What grievous task have you been given that could not display the handiwork of heaven if you submitted it to the Holy Spirit? Dream of elevating the mundane. Lean into it. The Spirit will give new life to everything you do. The Word will become flesh within you.

This is what Scripture means when it speaks of the fruit of the Spirit (see Gal. 5:22–23). It is the evidence of spiritual growth as an outcome of work.

GRILL MASTER

In the book of Acts, the Apostles were inspired by their calling to go and make disciples (see Matt. 28:19–20). But the practical demands of seeing to the needs of a community several thousand strong began to intrude on that great work. They decided that waiting on tables at the local food bank wasn't the best use of their time. "The twelve summoned the full number of the disciples and said, 'It is not right that we should give up preaching the word of God to serve tables'" (Acts 6:2).

Apparently croutons and Christ had different priorities in their minds. They were, after all, capital-*A* Apostles. So they put out a résumé request to find some waitstaff who would fit the bill. Their job description for a holy waiter is a revelation. As the Bible records, the minimum requirement for serving steak at their establishment was that the person be known to be "full of the Spirit and of wisdom" (Acts 6:3). Never mind past restaurant experience or the ability to balance trays laden with plates. No, what they cared about was the person's spiritual maturity. Of course! How else could the work be done well?

A young man named Stephen fit the role of God's grill master perfectly. Scripture says he was "full of grace and power [and] was doing great wonders and signs among the people" (Acts 6:8). You can believe he had more on his side than just a George Foreman grill.

There is no role too small for the Spirit to effect change in. No matter what job we have, the Father's requirement for any kind of work is the same as the one that applied to Stephen: we must be full of God's Spirit and of wisdom.

This wisdom isn't something we go out and generate on our own. Even this is a gift from God. What an incredible promise it is that he gives wisdom "generously to all without reproach" (James 1:5). In the book of Romans, Paul even said God gives us gifts "without repentance" (11:29 KJV), meaning he will never take them back. He never turns the library lights off on us! As much as we need to know about what we need to do, he'll teach us. How about that for a corporate training program?

Now, practically, what do signs and wonders have to do with flipping burgers? Absolutely nothing. Which, of course, shows us

God's sense of humor. He uses the small things to manifest his power. With him, the Spirit and the spatula go hand in hand.

WAKE UP

His invitation to us is to let him redeem the workday. So show up. Baby step numero uno is that we have to be physically there at the job. Every task is perfect for his power to work through. We simply have no excuse not to find purpose in our jobs. The first way we submit to the Potter's hand is to take personal ownership of the day he's given us.

Start by being present. In this way, you actively agree with him that the day is ready to be filled with the outpouring of his Spirit through the vessel of your life. Being expectant that he will fulfill his promises starts in the morning.

Imagine not showing up for work on time on a consistent basis. Would it go unnoticed? Probably not. But many Christians have neglected to show up for work spiritually. We need to remember that a paycheck is not the only thing we're working for.

God's mercies are new and available to us every morning (see Lam. 3:22–23). Even Monday mornings. We have not been given a job without the tools to accomplish it. God's faithfulness is something we should be taking advantage of. Apparently we are in need of a refill every twenty-four hours.

Start your daily labor by humbly recognizing that everything has been prepared for you. Be grateful that you are equipped with wisdom and enabled by grace. What a wonderful God you work for! Never in the history of the earth has there been a better foreman to be under. Under his leadership you can wake up with exceeding confidence, expecting him to show up in the details of every hour. In that kind of scenario, you might even get slightly saddened by having to knock off for lunch, as you're aching to see him effect change through the work of your hands. (But never fear: you can see him work through you at lunch too!) What a wonderful gift!

The workday is overflowing with promise, and all you have to do is be the vessel that catches it. You've already been given a holy advance and deposit for the day. Willingly give your best to whatever job or boss you serve.

A FAMILIAR MIRACLE

"I'm going out to fish," Simon Peter said (John 21:3 NIV).

What else was there to do? His Messiah was gone. The fun was over. His career calling, by extension, might just as well have been moot. At least fishing was a job that put food on the table—even if it felt less important spiritually.

Who could blame him? Any responsible man might do the same thing, given the circumstances. Life has priorities, after all.

Is this where life has caught you? You've walked with the Lord and experienced his goodness, but maybe family life has gotten stressful. Your sense of spiritual significance at work is at an all-time low. Or maybe your new role at work doesn't seem to fit quite right.

Perhaps you've just been doing the same thing for a long time and don't know how to make a change. Whatever the case, your work has had to become your top priority.

Imagine Peter's thoughts as he pushed out into the water to fish, ready to clock in for another day: *Maybe my experiences with Jesus are meant to be momentary. Maybe this was just a side trip we all took for a few years. Perhaps his claims really were too good to be true.*

Then someone on shore cut into his reverie: "Friends, haven't you any fish?" (v. 5 NIV).

"No," Peter replied. *I've been fishing all night with no success—that's my work life now.*

Undeterred, the voice continued: "Throw your net on the right side of the boat and you will find some" (v. 6 NIV).

Peter complied, though perhaps halfheartedly. Just days earlier, he'd been a fisher of men. Talk about a job with purpose! Now he was casting nets for ordinary fish.

But then, in response to his cast, a familiar miracle happened (see Luke 5:4–7). The net bulged and sagged. It was so full of fish it couldn't even be hauled into the boat.

Jesus was near. Something was shifting. Both the fish and the fisherman were being pulled in response to the call.

The same can be true for you. Jesus will meet you in your work, just as he met me when I was mowing my family's lawn. He will invite you into his work.

Are you willing to simply cast your net?

Daily Prayer

Father, thank you for equipping me for the day and for providing the grace I need to effect change in my daily work.

I look forward to working with you, to seeing the mundane made meaningful, to partnering with you in the practical and profound work of your kingdom.

Thank you for never failing to give me wisdom for what the day requires of me. Specifically I thank you for giving me wisdom for

_____.

Father, steady my hands and quiet my heart.

In the hard moments of the day, remind my soul that the playing field is even in Christ. I believe that all things, from promotion to provision, come from your hand.

Teach me today to work faithfully with you and for you.

I'm happy to spend the day alongside you.

In Christ, amen.

Chapter 2

THE STRENGTH AND THE WILL

The LORD turned to him and said, "Go in the strength you have and save Israel out of Midian's hand. Am I not sending you?"

—Judges 6:14 NIV

Enter Gideon, 1162 BC.

We find him in the book of Judges, a mama's boy two steps away from baking brownies with an Easy-Bake Oven (see 6:11–16). He was hiding the flour he'd made in a winepress. He was afraid of the invading Midianite army, who might steal his glorious gluten.

As the story unfolds, the Lord showed up, asked him to stop the muffin making, and instructed him to save Israel from their oppressors.

Gideon's response?

Fear.

Instead of opportunity, Gideon saw opposition. He questioned God's involvement in his family history. After all, Gideon's dad didn't follow Yahweh (see v. 25). Neither was Gideon from a military background. And he wasn't convinced that all the old stories regarding the deliverance of Egypt were entirely true. In his mind, neither he nor anyone in his family was cut out for the job.

God's response? "Go in the strength you have" (v. 14 NIV).

No *but*s. No *how*s. "Go in the strength you have." Gideon had only one option. But it was a good one.

"Am I not sending you?" (v. 14 NIV). The Lord promised to go before him (see v. 16).

Apparently this assurance clinched it for Gideon. He traded in his apron for a called career. He was still afraid, but he was also willing to do the hard work of putting one foot in front of the other.

In other words, he decided to man up.

THE STRENGTH I HAD

I was contemplating suicide. I'd been in depression for months. One day I wound up on my bed, sobbing and surrounded by pills. The idea of ending everything was not normal for me, but I had been through a really rough patch.

I had lost my car in a wreck. My cell phone had been turned off multiple times for nonpayment. I had lost access to the internet, my only source of income. My laptop had developed a faulty electrical cord, so I had no way to charge it to find out if some work did eventually come in. To top everything off, I had done a night in jail for some red-light tickets I couldn't afford to pay.

"Lord," I prayed in desperation, "I want to be on a team again." He responded.

I landed an interview at a software company. It was in two days, and I had to take a résumé. I was underqualified, so my hopes were not high. But it was an interview, and there wasn't exactly a line of eager companies wanting to hire me.

I have to admit to some reluctance even to go to the interview. If I got the job, it would mean a change. My life was not great, but it had some good parts. My rent was only $200 a month, and I had a TV. For some reason, those things made me feel settled and comfortable. Or maybe I was just afraid to be rejected again. Besides, how could I ready my résumé without even a working computer—much less get up to speed on the skills this job would require? It would be so much easier just to stay in my room.

Sometimes the decision to make a decision can be quite hard.

Nevertheless, I decided I would go in the strength I had.

I had two days to prepare, so I knew I had to get creative. First, the laptop needed to be fixed. I had no tools, but I did have a butter knife and some Scotch tape. These constituted the strength I had. They wouldn't make Bill Gates proud, but MacGyver … maybe.

With the laptop fixed, I needed to solve the internet issue. My only choice was to walk to the nearest Starbucks, about five miles away. Granted, this journey wasn't through the Sahara, but walking that distance in boots in the summer certainly made the struggle feel real. But I put on my (big boy) boots and made the trek.

With these problems solved and with me sitting in my booth at Starbucks, it was time to cram. I had only forty-eight hours to get myself up to speed, so I spent hours watching online classes, downloading ebooks, and giving myself tests on the content I was learning.

The work paid off.

I went to the interview, nailed it, and within a week was offered a salary above the US median income.

To an outsider, this might simply look like a little bit of hustle, not an act of God's mercy. I had gone in the strength I had, but the result was in the hands of the Almighty. Can a man take credit for the drive or work ethic he has been given?

SERVING THE BOSS AS IF SERVING THE LORD

The angel of the Lord presented Gideon with an opportunity. He could've refused the invitation, and he had enough doubts and fears that we might not have been surprised to see him do so. But he felt assured that God would be with him, so he willingly took ownership of the opportunity. He didn't feel particularly enthused at first, but he surrendered his will to the will of the Lord anyway.

How can you and I steward opportunities the way Gideon did? How do we go in the strength we have?

It starts with ownership. Ownership is a measuring stick that gauges the level of belief you have in the purpose and urgency of your work. If you bring a low level of ownership to your job, it means you hold the work you've been given in low esteem. It means you don't care, and that reflects on you. But a high level of ownership demonstrates a high level of caring about your work.

This makes sense to most of us. If we feel our work to be important, we value it more. If we respect those who have asked us to do a job, we may value it even a little more. If those things are lacking, we may value the job less, and that shows in our work. You might keep working hard for "the man." But if you don't, so what? The work wasn't that important anyway.

That's a natural way to think about a job. It's our culture's way. It's an attitude that's been around for centuries.

But it's not the way a Christian man is to think about his work. Let's look at Paul's advice to the men of Ephesus:

> Bondservants, obey your earthly masters with fear and trembling, with a sincere heart, as you would Christ, not by the way of eye-service, as people-pleasers, but as bondservants of Christ, doing the will of God from the heart, rendering service with a good will as to the Lord and not to man, knowing that whatever good anyone does, this he will receive back from the Lord, whether he is a bondservant or is free. (Eph. 6:5–8)

Christian men should desire to obey God with goodwill no matter what their role, status, or task. To this end, ownership keeps our hearts and minds present to what God might have us do during the day. You could be a CEO or a custodian, and God is still asking you to render service with the same level of commitment. With every boss we have. With every job we have. With all the strength we have.

Your goal should be to be wrung dry of every drop of love and goodwill you have in you. Every day. Rinse and repeat. This is the practical part of spiritual discipline. This is our part in it, the part where we go in the strength we have. The battle always belongs to the Lord, but we still have to show up for it. We still take ownership of the calling. Just as our brother Gideon did.

When a Christian man does his work in a spirit of ownership, it is like a magnet for God's presence. Ownership invites the Holy Spirit close because ownership agrees with his position on labor.

From day one, Gideon was meant to experience the provision and victory of the Lord in his new role. But if he'd never followed through, if he'd refused to believe God or to become a steward of the opportunity, his story would not have been of biblical proportions.

Ownership is faithful application of the strength you have.

Going in your strength is a precursor to faith-filled work.

You do your work by faith, or you don't. Same as you live. But that choice is always up to you. Paul wrote, "To me to live is Christ, and to die is gain. If I am to live in the flesh, that means fruitful labor for me" (Phil. 1:21–22). The aim of a Christian man is to be full of fruitful labor. His sweat should be soul spurred and Spirit filled.

There should be no career gaps in Christ. All the work we do should be done "as to the Lord and not to man" (Eph. 6:7). On our spiritual work résumé, there should not be any time when the work we've done has not been as to the Lord.

Jesus said we'd do greater things than him (see John 14:12), because he knew that the promised Holy Spirit would soon live in us, enabling further work by God on the earth through his followers. The Christian man at work is, in a sense, Jesus in that workplace. The man with the Holy Spirit in him has become both word and flesh. We're not Jesus incarnate, but we have Jesus on board with us, and that makes everything we do sacred and of divine importance.

Consequently, your job is, first and foremost, a labor of love.

If you bring the presence of Jesus to your workplace, I think you can see that showing up is not enough. Punching a time card is now a spiritual discipline.

Gideon answered the call (he showed up). But then he had to release control of that call. He had to follow God's instructions to take into battle an army of three hundred faithful men rather than the army of thirty-two thousand functional men he'd started with (see Judg. 7).

You have to do the same. You must invite the Holy Spirit to empower your reliance on him. Ask him to show you what tasks require his guidance, inspiration, and direction.

This is what a called man does. He recognizes and owns his position, whatever it may be, and he relies completely on the One who gave him the job to begin with.

By the way, complete reliance really does mean complete reliance. The Spirit needs access to your entire job. If you are wondering what parts of your work need more practical faith, ask yourself what tasks or people cause you the most stress.

Bingo. That tightness in your chest is an indication that the kingdom hasn't yet come into that part of your day. Invite the Lord into it now. Ask him to bring revelation to what is stressing you out. Revelation is simple, so don't let the idea feel condemning to you. God wants you to know how to live, so he brings practical, easy-to-understand instructions. In other words, you'll know what to do.

After you've prayed, ask yourself, "How do I do this work as unto God?" You do your work either as unto yourself, as unto your stress, or—hopefully—as unto your Father in heaven. When you do your work as unto God, you're agreeing with him that both the abilities he gave you and the opportunity in front of you can be used to accomplish his ends. This is the strength always available to you. This is how you own the day.

Having a called career is not about using human effort to produce impressive results. From God's perspective, there's no need to accomplish great things in your own power. Nor should you work really hard and then ask God to bless what you wanted to do anyway, in the hope that he'll push your output to an even higher level of excellence. Human excellence is simply the starting point where you begin to make yourself available to what a called career can offer you. For the Christian man, excellence requires that you are present spiritually, and being present spiritually puts all other priorities into godly alignment. Excellence shows our high esteem for the jobs God has given us to do.

Begin today. Build a list of heaven-sent ways to elevate the work you do. Perhaps it's speaking in a certain way, restructuring a process, or organizing teams differently in your company. As you bring these matters to God in prayer, you will begin to have ideas like this.

FIRMLY PLANTED

I would be willing to guess that every man who has ever had a job has felt hopeless at some point about the work he does. Remember that even Gideon felt lost and uncertain—both before and after he was called by God.

David once asked himself, "Why, my soul, are you downcast? Why so disturbed within me? Put your hope in God" (Ps. 43:5 NIV). Translation: "Your desperation is misguided, David. Pull it together." He commanded his inner man to participate in the Maker's reality. He told himself to act in accordance with the reality of his calling.

You can do the same—you can command your inner man when you feel as if you don't have any strength to go on. If you are feeling downcast, hopeless, or disturbed about your job, pull it together. God has made us this promise:

> How blessed is the man who does not walk in the
> counsel of the wicked,
> Nor stand in the path of sinners,
> Nor sit in the seat of scoffers!
> But his delight is in the law of the LORD,
> And in His law he meditates day and night.
> *He will be like a tree firmly planted by streams of water,*

Which yields its fruit in its season
And its leaf does not wither;
And in whatever he does, he prospers.
                        (Ps. 1:1–3 NASB)

The Christian man is firmly planted in his spot by God. The further you lean into God's truth, the truer it will show itself to be. The more you inspect the corners and edges of a promise, the more practical divinity you'll find in it.

Ask yourself,

- Do I believe I'm firmly planted (see the passage above)?
- Do I believe I'm predestined for good works (see Eph. 2:10)?
- Do I believe the Almighty will complete the good work he started in me (see Phil. 1:6)?
- If God, who called me into existence to be a steward of his kingdom, calls me to works that are in keeping with repentance, to overcome my flesh through the inner working of his Spirit, by the power of his Word and the intentionality of his love, how will he not establish me?

David's heart inspired him to write that we are "fearfully and wonderfully made" (Ps. 139:14). Do you agree with him? God is still waiting for shepherds to see themselves as kings and for laymen and leaders alike to fear the Lord. All men should recognize that they are seated in heavenly places (see Eph. 2:6), able to do their daily work from a higher perspective.

Do you agree?

Your job—regardless of your role, title, or wealth—is to dedicate the work of your hands to building his kingdom. This begins within your working hours, every working day, by being spiritually present and accounted for.

No collar color has a higher calling than another. We are all slaves and kings—slaves to Christ and reigning kings—born into a royal priesthood. In the end, we will all cast our crowns before the Almighty (see Rev. 4:10).

How far you throw your crown in this lifetime is a matter of stewardship. See yourself as Gideon finally did: fully capable of living out your calling, since God is the one who called you to it. No gift is too small and no background is too broken for you to find purpose in your work through finding purpose in him.

In Christ you have been given abundant life (see John 10:10). This promise is richer than any financial raise or promotion, and it's greater than any sense of the unknown. When your hands are working for the Lord, you can effect as much change with a push broom as a president can with a pen.

The questions, then, brother, are these: Where are your hands, and what are they committed to? In other words, how present are you *spiritually* to the work already in front of you?

A LABOR OF LOVE

The Lord called Gideon. The Lord has also called you.

Your daily work may not feel connected to a divine calling, but rest assured, it is. If he has called you, he will sustain you. You are clay in the Potter's hands. He's designing you with a purpose. He's making you into a tool to be used in specific situations for a certain kind of work. The sooner you see and agree with the shape of the tool or vessel he's making you to be, the faster you will become comfortable with the purpose he has made you for.

This should give you great joy: you were made for a work purpose, and he will sustain you.

I love this verse by Paul: "It is before his own master that [a man] stands or falls. And he will be upheld, for the Lord is able to make him stand" (Rom. 14:4). What a powerful promise that is!

Do you feel it? Can you sense his guiding voice saying, "Son, I will make you stand"? He is making you stand right now, in this very moment, and he will make you stand tomorrow when the moment has passed. That's the promise you receive when your way is committed to him. Be fully convinced of it. Even when you doubt that you're capable of being called to do God's work, he has promised to equip you in every possible way to make you capable of partnership with him (see 2 Cor. 9:8). The way you show God that you believe that promise is to obediently show up and be present with whatever strength you possess.

The Lord will make you stand in the work you do, because that is part of how he's sanctifying you. That is the wonderful work of salvation: it goes from glory to glory (see 2 Cor. 3:18). He will not forget you in your working hours. He does not sanctify just two-thirds of your day and leave out the rest. "In him we live and move and have our being" (Acts 17:28).

So cast off doubt that God has called you to your work. Go in the strength you have. Be present and bring excellence as you do your job as if you were working directly for Jesus. Your success is not a numbers game. It's as easy for God to win a battle with three hundred men as with thirty-two thousand. It's as easy for him to resurrect Lazarus as to raise the entire bride of Christ at once (see John 11:43–44). It is not a matter of effort for him—only intention. Surely it is no great stretch for him to take the toil of your day and cause it to bear good things.

What the Lord called Gideon to do, the Lord sustained him through. This is a promise for every man who does the will of God. You included. You may never have a visitation like Gideon's, but your command is the same: "Go in the strength you have."

Your response may be the same as well: "Who—me? But I have no strength. At least not the kind I think God wants or can do any-thing with." But by accepting the call, you participate in the call. We tend to view the path of calling and its destination differently. "How am I supposed to accomplish something for the Lord?" you might ask. "I don't even know what that would look like."

Good news: you never need to.

With Gideon, God had two outcomes in mind: Israel's victory and Gideon's participation in that victory. This was true before God visited Gideon. This was true when Gideon was hiding. This was true when Gideon had to manage an army. This was also true when the final victory had been won.

The man of God simply had to step into his responsibility. To own every step. As long as he was in obedience, Gideon was operating in the calling he was given. This led to greater and greater work and responsibility along the way. Not to mention better stories of the Lord's involvement. That can be your story too.

Daily Prayer

Father, I agree with you. I agree that you have called me to lead with excellence and servant-heartedness in everything I do. I will leave no stone unturned as I look for opportunities to allow your kingdom to come into the minutes of my day. I'll go in the strength you've given me, full of expectancy for the day.

Specifically I ask that you show me a new way of approaching _____. I want the work I do to give witness to you. Not just my attitude about it, but the work itself as well. Show me your ways that I may walk in them. Give me your mind that I may act wisely.

Just as with your servant Gideon, show me when thirty-two thousand reasons for confidence won't add up. I ask that you prompt my spirit when I begin to put confidence in my flesh instead of in you. I desire to live a life full of practical faith, especially today.

In Christ, amen.

Chapter 3

THE URGENCY AND THE OPPORTUNITY

"All flesh is like grass and all its glory like the flower of grass. The grass withers, and the flower falls, but the word of the Lord remains forever." And this word is the good news that was preached to you.

—1 Peter 1:24–25

I was on top of the world, though I was far from the heights of my spiritual goals.

The Fountain Place skyscraper is 720 feet above the street, and my job was to clean the roofs of every major skyscraper in Dallas. Birds flew below me. Even clouds sometimes passed below where I was working. My altitude was high, but I was well beneath where I wanted to be spiritually.

Three days a week, I would wake up at five in the morning, grab a doughnut, and make the trek to the big city. I felt invisible to the crowds around me. I worked with my eyes pointed downward, and I was usually covered in grime and asphalt. But I couldn't have been happier. I was making fifteen dollars an hour, and it felt like manna raining from heaven. God had provided work for me, and I walked in constant gratitude.

But gratitude was not what I'd been feeling only a couple of weeks before. More like desperation and fear.

Not long before I took the city job, I had transitioned out of a full-time ministry, where I'd been working for a local church. In my naïveté, I left the church job and headed to the big city with stars in my eyes ... but without having lined up any replacement for the lost income.

Because I didn't really know what I should be doing with my life, I was in limbo. Actually I was in Dallas, an expensive city to live in, without a steady job and with growing anxiety. Quickly I had to shift into survival mode, looking for jobs anywhere, even day-labor work, and this took up most of my energy.

I remember sitting in a pizzeria in the middle of the afternoon, forcing myself to enjoy every bite because I didn't know how much longer I could afford to eat. In mid chew I heard God's voice: "I'm going to let you down easy."

I felt immediate peace and comfort. I understood him to mean that he hadn't forgotten or abandoned me and that he was going to take care of me. That inner voice was a light to my path and a direct deposit to my soul. For the moment the worry was gone.

"Lord," I prayed, "I need a job."

The next day I ran into a buddy whom I hadn't seen in months. His first words, half a step from hello, were "Do you need a job?"

I was so stunned it took me a minute to answer. "Um, yes."

"Hold on. Let me make a call."

I think I held my breath for the entire five minutes of his phone call.

He put his phone away and nodded. "Can you start tomorrow?"

I felt as if my feet had been set on solid ground. Of course I could start tomorrow! The next day I was hired to clean the roofs of skyscrapers, and suddenly I could afford to have pizza every night of the week if I wanted it.

I can't tell you how all this rejuvenated my faith. God had spoken to me about a job, and he had quickly acted on his promise. The work itself was irrelevant—what was important was that God had gone before me.

It was as if God had a specific plan for what job he wanted me to have.

He was present. He was *for* me. He had heard my prayer and come to my rescue. So I didn't care whether the job was fixing sidewalks, flipping burgers, or mucking out stables—he was worthy of my best efforts in the work he'd given me to do.

The Lord used that time to shape my perspective about what work could be for the Christian. Early in the morning I would get up and plan what I wanted to do with my life. As it turned out, it wouldn't be too many years later that I began to rise to the tops of buildings like the ones I had cleaned the roofs of.

FIND MEANING IN ANY JOB

I'd never seen myself as a concrete-repair guy. I actually didn't care for the work that much. But when your perspective is one of deep gratitude, any job feels like a blessing right from the hand of the Almighty.

As you grow in the awareness that you are at this job as Jesus' employee, you will begin to see the scaffolding of kingdom work all around you. You'll see that God has work orders written up for the people, relationships, team culture, and leadership you encounter in the office or at the work site. And you'll understand that this is why God has brought a man such as yourself to this job.

I found an amazing illustration of how to spot God's meaning in any job in a surprising place: the Old Testament story of when the queen of Sheba paid a visit to King Solomon (see 1 Kings 10:1–13).

This was no ordinary diplomatic visit. Solomon's reputation for wisdom had spread far beyond the boundaries of his kingdom, and world leaders were beginning to take notice.

One of the heads of state who heard of Solomon's wisdom was the queen of Sheba. She mounted a huge expedition, led by her royal self, and trekked from Sheba (which was either in southern Arabia or in modern-day Ethiopia) to Jerusalem, Solomon's capital.

Solomon received her with all the pomp her position deserved, and the two monarchs consulted. In these sessions the queen asked him "all that was on her mind" (v. 2) and "Solomon answered all her questions" (v. 3), including about the matters that had perplexed both her and her counselors.

Needless to say, the queen was blown away by Solomon's wisdom. And then, when she thought she couldn't learn anything more, Solomon invited her to a royal feast. At that banquet everything the queen saw, down to the table arrangements, took her breath away.

> When the queen of Sheba had seen all the wisdom of Solomon, the house that he had built, the food of his table, the seating of his officials, and the attendance of his servants, their clothing, his cupbearers, and his burnt offerings that he offered at the house of the LORD, there was no more breath in her. (vv. 4–5)

What was it about Solomon's presentation at this banquet that moved the queen of Sheba so much?

I've identified six principles related to Solomon's attitude toward work that we can learn and apply to any job we may have.

1. The House That Solomon Built

The first thing that took the queen's breath away about Solomon's banquet was the house he'd built for himself.

Solomon built his own house. He didn't move into someone else's domain. He defined the context he lived in. He built his context from the ground up. The king took ownership of his environment. He took responsibility for his surroundings.

You know how to manage your home well. Now take that same intentionality to your workplace. If you want to find your calling in whatever job you have, then for you there can be no such thing as "That's not my responsibility!" It's *your* place of work. It's all your responsibility.

That doesn't mean you're necessarily the boss, of course. But you should take care of the workplace as if it does belong to you. You should be sensitive to the needs of your coworkers as if they were family. If you see trash on the floor or a fire door blocked, you don't walk by, thinking *It's not my job to fix.* No, you walk around as if you own the place—in the sense of taking pride in it and responsibility for it.

What is under your trust at work that could be improved? Which organizational system or process needs to be built in a better way? What can you take ownership of that would further the organization's goals? Look for unowned opportunity in your workplace.

You will find meaning in your work as you take responsibility for its success.

2. The Food of His Table

The second thing the queen was impressed with was the food of Solomon's banquet table.

Some men are social creatures, loving to collaborate, synergize, and chat. Others long to be left alone. Taken to an unwise extreme, a desire for independence will isolate you. And isolation can be detrimental.

All around us are examples of Christian men who reach the pinnacle of success and then have a terrible fall. Almost always, it comes out later that the person had cut himself off from accountability. He had isolated himself, and in that secretiveness, sin had crept in.

Perhaps King Solomon was thinking of this when he instituted the practice of eating with others. Solomon made community—and perhaps a measure of accountability—a point of emphasis for him, even at his lofty place in life.

Here at his table, we see an invitation to abandon isolation. Many jobs must be done in silence or alone much of the time, but even in those we can invite others into what we're doing. We can make even daily routines, like breaks or lunch, group events. Doing so has multiple benefits for us as men.

First, we are better as a team. Even though it may not always feel comfortable, you are better off when you surround yourself with brothers.

Second, when what you do is done in public, your work is on display for all to see. After all, if you do good work, it will not go unnoticed. Sometimes doing good work in wise ways results in promotion, and that can be a blessing not only to you and your family but also to those you are then in a position to interact with in new ways.

So ask yourself, "Do I have enough people at my table?"

3. The Seating of Officials

The third thing that impressed the queen of Sheba was something about how Solomon arrayed his officials, ministers, advisers, and managers at the table. Or maybe it was *that* he had them at the table at all.

It's fascinating to me that Solomon, the wisest man in the world, surrounded himself with good counsel. Not long after Solomon ascended to the throne, God appeared to him in a dream and asked what gift Solomon desired. Rather than riches or long life, Solomon asked for wisdom to rule God's people well (see 1 Kings 3:5–14).

So why all the officials around him at the banquet? What good are counselors when you are the smartest man in the room—or the world?

There is a lesson here. Having the ability to accomplish a job well is great, but walking in humility is greater. Walking in humility *is* wisdom. As Christian men, the greater our capacity and expertise, the greater must be our humility. The more we understand and the better we are at what we do, the lower we must become.

Regardless of your role and how long you've been in it, you will always be in need of good counsel. You can't think of everything. You can't factor in multiple perspectives if yours is the only one you consider. This is true whether you own a business, are an entry-level employee, or are an executive in an ivory tower. If the wisest man in the world made sure he had the benefit of many advisers, I'm thinking it's a good idea for us too.

Again, doing so is both prudent for life and helpful on the practical side. Placing yourself under someone else's wise oversight is the quickest way to promotion, job protection, and long-term success. Plus, any important endeavor benefits from feedback. Solomon's words again: "Plans fail for lack of counsel, but with many advisers they succeed" (Prov. 15:22 NIV).

A banquet table populated with officials who are free to speak into your life is a great way to make sure you don't get too full of yourself. Every man needs someone (at least one person) who can tell him no. Someone who can call your bluff and inform your ignorance. This side of heaven, no one outgrows the need for counsel.

Contrary to common thought, the more successful you become, the more you need it. There is a myth in our culture that says the more someone is promoted, the less oversight that person needs. Or that the higher a man goes in his work, the more decisions he can make without consulting anyone.

That is one way great men can fall.

Start building an inner circle of confidants who support you spiritually and practically. Don't automatically pick only your old friends. Find men who can both speak as a father to you and inform your decision-making process.

Don't rest until you find good counsel. Not having it is the reason some men's blessings become Bathshebas.

4. Servants and Their Clothes

Something about "the attendance of [Solomon's] servants [and] their clothing" impressed the queen of Sheba (1 Kings 10:5). Perhaps it was the mutual honor shown by king and servants.

You cannot honor someone by accident. Honor is intentional. Solomon clothed his servants well, honoring their service with magnificent attire. In return, his servants honored Solomon.

No matter what job you have, you can clothe others with honor. You can treat your boss with honor. You can treat your peers with honor. And if you manage a team, you can treat your team members with honor. You can clothe your clients, suppliers, cooks, mail carriers, repair staff, drivers, security people, forklift operators, waiters, pilots, and dental hygienists with honor.

Think long and hard about the culture you want to have in your work environment. To the extent that it depends on you, clothe others with the honor you want everyone around you to wear.

Perhaps you don't oversee people directly or you exist in the ecosystem of a large organization. That's fine. You can still design the microculture of your cubicle. Or garage, work bay, or factory line. You're the one carrying the Holy Spirit—affect the room! Empower people in such a way that it causes those both inside and outside your immediate sphere to notice what you're clothing others in.

This is important kingdom work you can do in any job. And you can do it without preaching or handing out Bible verses. Clothe those around you in the atmosphere of heaven, and they'll be happy to work with you.

And maybe they'll start to wonder what you have that they don't.

5. Cupbearers

What was it about Solomon's cupbearers at that banquet that so impressed the queen?

When it comes to finding your calling in any job, I recommend you change the old saying "The Devil is in the details" to "Divinity is in the details."

The Hebrew word translated "cupbearers" can mean people who serve drinks (cupbearers, butlers, or waiters)—or it can mean the cups themselves. I like to think that the queen of Sheba was by this point so overwhelmed by Solomon's wisdom that she detected superior order even in the choice and arrangement of the cups and plates at the table.

When we see things marvelously arrayed, we know there was some incredible mind behind their creation. The order of the stars and planets reveals great might and wisdom. The majesty of the mountains reflects thought and a kind of divine project management. Sea currents point to intentional construction.

Ask yourself, "What could use my attention in this job? What detail, if it were elevated by heaven's wisdom, would direct and delight those around me? What around me could I do or change that would admirably represent Christ?"

6. The Offerings

The final thing about Solomon's banquet that took the queen's breath away was his offerings to God. Neither this monarch nor her realm revered the God of Israel, yet something about these offerings put her in such awe that she gave one of the great declarations of praise in the Bible:

> Blessed be the LORD your God, who has delighted
> in you and set you on the throne of Israel! Because
> the LORD loved Israel forever, he has made you
> king, that you may execute justice and righteous-
> ness. (1 Kings 10:9)

Today we are disconnected from the idea of sacrifices and offerings, especially in the sense of ritually slain animals. A *sacrifice*, in the
Old Testament, was required to pay the punishment for a sin committed before God. An *offering* was something different. Offerings
were voluntary. They were "just 'cause" gifts to God. An offering was
rooted in gratitude. It was a gift given above and beyond a person's
sacrifice.

Evidently, Solomon took this principle to heart. Even in a great
banquet to honor a foreign head of state, he kept Israel's gratitude
and devotion to God front and center.

The queen would've considered this remarkable and quite
countercultural. Throughout the Bible, there are examples of pagan
monarchs requiring that offerings be given to themselves. Golden
statues, royalty worship, and required tribute are all over their stories.

Solomon went the other direction. In fact, this was probably one
of the most powerful things the queen saw during her visit, if only
because it demonstrated how he, as someone in a privileged position,
saw his role as a grateful servant of God.

Do you see yourself as a grateful servant of God in your job?

Work should be a praise offering. The way we work with our
hands is the offering we give. Your grateful offering of work at your

job says more about you than any evangelistic tract or song sung on Sunday morning.

Say of any day at your job, "This is the day that the LORD has made" (Ps. 118:24). You cannot put your heart in a position of gratitude toward God and have a bad attitude toward the work you've been given. Try it today.

Gratitude for your job puts the focus back on God as the provider of your employment. I certainly felt that gratitude when I was given the opportunity (directly from God) to seal sidewalks.

When your focus is on God as the source of your job success, you will stand out among your peers. How often do you give your successes back to God? How often do you model worship in the workplace through an attitude of offering? I love this statement by Jesus: "Let your light shine before others, so that they may see your good works and give glory to your Father who is in heaven" (Matt. 5:16).

When you don't take credit for your successes but rather give the credit to God, you are saying something to those around you about who and what your life is about. This type of office-place offering will often say more about what you believe than any pamphlet or Jesus piece of jewelry ever could.

If you want to uncover meaning in any job and learn what else God has for you to do, treat your work the same way he treats his work. This is how you use "the mind of Christ" that Scripture talks about (1 Cor. 2:16). This is how Solomon was able, with supernatural help, to do more than be just another king. It's how his work pointed the queen toward God.

The queen of Sheba had "no more breath in her" when she saw Solomon's banquet (1 Kings 10:5), especially since he'd also dropped so much wisdom on her.

The great thing is that we can apply to our employment situations the same wise principles Solomon demonstrated in that feast. No matter what job we have, we can find our calling in our work as we (1) take responsibility for it as if the business were our own, (2) make sure we do not isolate ourselves, (3) get ourselves under the authority and accountability of wise counselors, (4) clothe those around us with honor, (5) elevate excellence in the details of our jobs, and (6) do our jobs with hearts full of gratitude toward God.

When we operate according to these six principles, we're treating our work with godly reverence and intensity. Another word for this is *urgency*. It's the primary way we engage our hearts to accept the mantle of our called career.

"Son, you need a sense of urgency." When I was a boy, my dad would say this to me whenever he wanted me to treat some task around the house with the same importance as he did. Some tasks are time sensitive. Some tasks are really important because they affect other people. Still others are meant to mature us into more skillful workers. The same is true for your calling.

Your Father God first provides you with a job, and then he waits to see how you treat that work before allowing you to partner with him on bigger things. This isn't punishment or cause for concern; it's just the natural order of supernatural work. Hammers before jackhammers. Plumb lines before power tools. Agreement with God before awakening in calling. So often we think of our current jobs as if they have nothing to do with our calling, so we don't approach them with the reverence they deserve. We'll never discover our holy work with this attitude.

Jobs are provided supernaturally by God's hand. When we revere God in that work, honor it as holy, and treat it with intention, it demonstrates to him that we're ready for what we are really meant to do. That ought to bring an importance—an urgency—to whatever job you have.

This is spiritual urgency. It is agreeing with God that the task right in front of you requires an earnest and persistent attitude. This attitude in and of itself will give new meaning to your work—though it's really just the start of all that's in store for you. After all, as we've seen from Solomon, all kinds of things can awake in others a deep desire for God.

God is looking for you to understand that every moment of your workday—even the mundane parts—is ripe for action. This is the same attitude that great men of the faith had by the time they were in the middle of their own called careers.

With these things in mind, you can find purpose in any job, not just "holy" jobs or jobs that make you a "professional Christian." Even if you put this book down right now, you will have gotten the premise of it.

But there's another way to look at the Bible that will escalate the work you do from the level of meaningful to the level of urgent.

A HOPEFUL EXPECTATION

Jesus is coming again. We don't know the day or the hour, of course, but the Bible is clear that the awareness of his imminent return ought to be in our minds, giving urgency to everything we do.

For the Christian man, the reality of Christ's coming is the under-current beneath every calling and job. We all desire God's will to be done on earth just as it is in heaven (see Matt. 6:10). Since we don't know when Jesus might return or even what might happen and in what order, the desire to spread his message ought to become the driving force for what a Christian man does during any day, at work or at home or wherever he is. (We still have to do our actual jobs too!)

The opportunity we have as Christian men is to look out over the world and see it as Jesus does: as a field ready for harvest (see John 4:35). God sees humanity—including that portion you interact with at your job—as being full of potential. He has strategically set you in this time and place, not to mention this place of employment, for just such a time as this.

One thing the sobering reality of Jesus' return may do is clarify for us what is important. It ought to give us a clear sense of what is useless, hamster-wheel work and what is work that will endure. How much time do we have to tell our family, friends, and coworkers about Christ before it's too late?

This awareness of our finite opportunity to share the good news ought to give our jobs—whatever they are—a new urgency. Talk about finding meaning in your work!

This urgency will lead us to manifest him throughout our workday.

When the Christian man goes to work, he is colaboring with Christ in the expectation of his return. You cannot overlook it. God is "not willing that any should perish" (2 Pet. 3:9 KJV). This truth makes any job an urgent, critical, meaningful, purposeful, mission-related job.

It gives you your calling.

An expectation that Jesus' return could happen at any moment is a great lens for looking at all your labor and discerning what needs to be done more, what needs to be done less, and what needs to be undone. Paul said it like this:

> No one can lay a foundation other than that which is laid, which is Jesus Christ. Now if anyone builds on the foundation with gold, silver, precious stones, wood, hay, straw—each one's work will become manifest, for the Day will disclose it, because it will be revealed by fire, and the fire will test what sort of work each one has done. If the work that anyone has built on the foundation survives, he will receive a reward. If anyone's work is burned up, he will suffer loss, though he himself will be saved, but only as through fire. (1 Cor. 3:11–15)

In other words, your work matters. No matter what job you have, Paul said you are a builder. If you're a cook, you're building with gold or wood. If you're an accountant, you're building with silver or straw. Let's build with the best materials—what do you say? That means having your mind set on demonstrating Christ to those you encounter wherever you spend time.

We don't know what day or hour the Lord will return. Neither do we know how many days we have on earth if Jesus tarries. In our jobs—and all the parts of our lives—we need to live in light of the possibility that we may not have a tomorrow to talk to our coworkers, bosses, or employees about eternal life.

AMALGAMATION

We all work for something. At some points in our lives, we might work just to survive, as I was doing all those years ago in downtown Dallas. At some points, we might work to pay off debt, feed a family, save for a vacation, prove a point, return a favor, buy a car, undo a mistake, turn over a new leaf, or just keep the lights on and the fridge semistocked.

The six principles we saw in Solomon's life will help you approach work with a godly mind-set, and the expected return of Christ will give urgent purpose to any job. With these tools, you'll be ready to start moving into greater and more meaningful work.

Part of finding purpose in your work is not trying to glorify yourself by using every scheme to get ahead, by fighting for your way at the office, or by wallowing in the muck of water-fountain politics. You really don't want to step into the boxing ring with the Holy Spirit and start trading punches for who deserves glory.

No matter how many accolades you receive, they will fade. Your bank account will eventually empty. Your nameplates and plaques will be taken off the walls and replaced with new ones.

When we work for wrong reasons, we can often find ourselves thinking, *Why is the day so long?* But when we're living out our calling—embracing the meaning in our work and living with the urgency of limited time—the cry of our hearts becomes *Why is the day so short?*

And our prayer becomes "God, grant me the revelation to squeeze every drop out of these eight short hours."

When I got that job cleaning the roofs of skyscrapers in Dallas, I knew God had plans for me. I approached that job, which others might not have cared for, as if it was a blessing from the hand of Jesus himself, which it was. When we bring that sort of gratitude and perspective, any job becomes a ministry job.

No one knows the amount of time he has on this earth. But you have been given an incredible gift: the opportunity to share your life, through what you do for a living, with your Maker. There is simply no better way to spend the day.

Make the most of it.

Daily Prayer

Father, grant me the wisdom to prioritize the parts of my day. Show me the details that don't have heaven on them yet. Reveal to me the low-hanging fruit that will give you glory. I want to live courageously. I want your Spirit to spur my sense of urgency. Teach me to number my days (see Ps. 90:12). Show me what deserves my time, and remove the dross of everything that doesn't.

Like Solomon, I need your wisdom. I can't navigate the day without the indwelling of your Spirit. Fill me with consciousness. Make my heart aware of the things you see. I want to see that the micro and macro tasks during the day have your thumbprint on them. I want others to see that mark of your presence. Glorify yourself in me and make me like you. Come over my thought processes in new and delightful ways. I long to spend the day with you.

Let's get started!

In Christ, amen.

Chapter 4

THE KNOWLEDGE
AND THE ANOINTING

The LORD said to Moses, "See, I have called by name Bezalel
the son of Uri, son of Hur, of the tribe of Judah, and I
have filled him with the Spirit of God, with ability and
intelligence, with knowledge and all craftsmanship."

—Exodus 31:1–3

I was surrounded by suits in a high-profile boardroom. The CEO,
CMO, and other executives of the packaging company my team was
assisting all had their eyes on me, waiting for me to solve their sizable
dilemma. Their sales had dropped considerably and the company
was suffering. We had identified several causes, from internal politics
to a lack of industry education. So far their sales team hadn't been
able to overcome those hurdles with their buyers.

Frankly, we were stumped. One or more causes remained hidden from us, and all the keen minds in the room couldn't see what they might be. I'd always been good at planning and problem-solving. But my natural abilities failed me this time.

Happily, as Christians, we're not limited to natural abilities.

So, with the whiteboard in front of me and all eyes on my back, I asked the Lord what to do. I shut my eyes and practiced some serious active listening.

Instantly he put a plan into my mind and soul. I clearly saw the errors in communication that had caused customers to become confused. More importantly, I suddenly knew what to do about the problem. I even saw in my head a diagram I could draw to illustrate the solution. In an amazing supernatural download, God impressed on me the eight pillars of the client's business and how they needed to be organized. He then showed me how to connect those pillars to the organization's overall mission.

I scribbled feverishly on the whiteboard, praising God with every dry-erase squeak. Once I wrote everything out, I presented it.

You should've seen the lightbulbs go on over the heads in that room. The client's leadership team loved what I'd shown them and were enthusiastically on board with bringing it to pass. My team worked with the client company to put together the business assets they'd need to be effective, and we were off to the races.

That experience was fun and completely exhilarating. However, aside from praising God for his help and being overjoyed that we'd been able to help our clients, I didn't think much of it.

But a month later, we received a call from the company's CEO. It turned out that the communication approach we'd outlined had opened up entirely new conversations for their company. Now they were talking business with the likes of General Mills and Smucker's. The CEO was thrilled, and of course, we were overjoyed.

On one level, I was very pleased and not a little amazed. But on the other, I'd come to understand that such things are no big deal for the Almighty.

This kind of partnership with God is normal—and even to be expected—when you work in your *anointing*. Although, for you, partnership through anointing may look different. Anointing is a custom-fit gift from Christ.

MY WHAT, NOW?

In Bible times, anointing was simply what you called it when you poured something onto something else. Like maybe you poured a liquid onto leather to make it more durable or weatherproof. Or maybe you poured a medicinal ointment onto a wound. Shepherds anointed the heads of their sheep with oil to protect them from bugs.

God instructed Jewish priests or prophets to pour oil onto the head of a person to show that he had been set aside for holy purposes. When David was still a shepherd boy, the prophet Samuel anointed him—poured oil onto his head—to signify that God had chosen him to be the future king of Israel (see 1 Sam. 16:13). Jesus was known as the Messiah and the Christ. *Messiah* means "anointed one" in Hebrew, and *Christ* means "anointed" in Greek.

In some Christian circles today, anointing is thought of in strictly spiritual terms. Some think anointing is a special empowerment by God's Spirit, either as a permanent blessing or as a touch for a certain moment. Others believe God's anointing comes and goes as the Holy Spirit sees needs arise, and still others believe that every Christian is anointed by definition and this anointing stays on the Christian until death.

For our purposes, let's understand anointing as the power of Christ poured out on you. This power sets you apart for godly, faith-filled living. And since work is part of that Christ-empowered lifestyle, we want to look at how anointing influences a job.

When I stood in that boardroom surrounded by suits and God downloaded not only the insights about what was going on but also the knowledge of what needed to be done, I acted from a position of anointing. He took what was already a natural ability of mine and elevated it to provide a breakthrough that none of the humans in the room would likely have had even if we'd stayed put for twenty years. I offered myself (including my skill set) to the Lord, and he used it in a mighty way that couldn't be otherwise explained.

Anointing is, in part, *talent that has been redeemed*. It is the breath of God enlivening a skill set. It is what happens to an ability that is offered for the Lord's purposes.

In one sense, every Christian is permanently anointed by God's Spirit. John described it this way in one of his letters:

> As for you, the anointing you received from him
> remains in you, and you do not need anyone to
> teach you. But as his anointing teaches you about
> all things and as that anointing is real, not coun-
> terfeit—just as it has taught you, remain in him.
> (1 John 2:27 NIV)

That's what happened to me in that boardroom. I didn't have any human there teaching me—the anointing from God brought the wisdom that was needed. This is the experience all Christian men can have on the job. And it can happen with more and more regularity. In fact, having an awareness of your anointing allows you to be bold in ways you might never dare to be otherwise. This, in turn, brings miraculous outcomes to your work.

A mind-blowing example of this comes from when I was in ministry.

ANOINTED FOR A TASK

The fuel light was on, and I had no money to pay for gas. Neither did the rest of the ministry team who were with me. Our Ford Windstar minivan wasn't exactly the poster child for fuel economy either.

Normally this wouldn't have been an issue. The missions organi-zation we worked for gave us a monthly fuel allowance. This month, however, there wasn't enough to go around. Sometimes we could scrape by or pool our funds, but this time we were at the end of what we could do through human means.

There has never been a time in my life when I truly had a need for work and the Lord didn't provide—through talent, time, or more obviously divine provision. The reality of him equipping me to do the job he's set before me has been proven to me many times. This allows me to come at challenges from a place of anointing and boldness. If I've been given the task by God, I know he'll provide the way for it to happen.

This was one of those times.

Before we got in the van, the team huddled to pray for gas money. We were getting in the vehicle and driving toward that ministry event, gas in the tank or not. This was nonnegotiable for us. We were committed to going. It would be up to God to get us there … on holy fumes or by teleportation maybe, but we were going.

By some miracle we made it to the event. Great things happened and God was glorified.

Then we had to get home. No angel had filled up the gas tank while we were inside. We still had no gas, and we needed to make it back to the church. We were worried. We needed another miracle. It seemed impossible, but we got in and headed out. Now it was not just our van but also our faith that was running on fumes.

We stopped at an intersection, and one of our teammates exclaimed, "There's money in the street!"

We thought he was joking. Sure. Like God would put unclaimed cash out on the street, right when we needed it.

He did.

And it wasn't chump change. Blowing along the street—some even going into the storm drain—were bills ranging from ones to twenties. Just fluttering everywhere, with no one in sight. There was no wallet, no bank bag, and no suitcase.

We jumped out of the van and grabbed the money as if we were in one of those phone-booth games with cash blowing all around. We collected forty-three dollars right from God's wallet.

Whenever anyone tells me, "Yeah, that'll happen when pigs fly," I reply, "Or when money blows in the wind?" and I tell that story.

The lesson for me was simple: God, in his grace, sets us apart for specific works. Then he makes sure we have everything we need to accomplish those works. This is the atmosphere of anointing. It lets you focus on your work without having to worry about how it will get done. That's God's part.

Did you know you have been anointed by God? Do you feel anointed? Most Christian men don't believe they're anointed. If they feel they have been set apart by God in any area, it might be in the realm of church or mission trips or telling people about Jesus. It might be in the sense of being commissioned to take care of a family. To put food on the table. To provide for a wife.

God's anointing remains (or *abides*) in you and teaches you about everything: who he is, how he saves, and how he'd like you to join in what he's doing in the world.

John said in his letter that Jesus' anointing teaches us about all things. And of course, "all things" *includes the work you do.*

Jesus was called, anointed, and set apart for God's service.

As a Christian, you too are set apart to be a servant, priest, and king. You had skills and talents before you came to Christ, but they were just human and natural. Without him, you had no sacred skill. But with his Spirit inside you, your skills are …

Anointed.

This anointing isn't just for your enjoyment (though, honestly, who wouldn't want to have what almost amounts to a superpower?). You've been saved and anointed for a reason. The anointing is the thing that sets you apart for a holy purpose.

God's anointing is on you because you have been set apart for certain tasks, many of which will be accomplished on the job. If your calling is the van you're driving to do the works God sets before you, then anointing is the fuel that will get you there.

BEZALEL AND OHOLIAB (GESUNDHEIT)

My favorite Bible story about how God anointed a man's skills for his purposes comes from the book of Exodus. God had led his people out of Egypt, and as he guided them to their new homeland, he taught them how to worship him. He instructed them to build a kind of traveling temple, called a tabernacle, to be the meeting place between God and people. Let's listen in:

> The LORD said to Moses, "See, I have called by name
> Bezalel the son of Uri, son of Hur, of the tribe of

> Judah, and I have filled him with the Spirit of God,
> with ability and intelligence, with knowledge and
> all craftsmanship, to devise artistic designs, to work
> in gold, silver, and bronze, in cutting stones for set-
> ting, and in carving wood, to work in every craft.
> And behold, I have appointed with him Oholiab,
> the son of Ahisamach, of the tribe of Dan. And I
> have given to all able men ability, that they may
> make all that I have commanded you." (31:1–6)

God had a big job for his people. They'd probably seen large structures, such as the pyramids in Egypt, but this work was unique. It needed to inspire people to revere God.

The Lord knew what to do, of course. He'd raised up Bezalel and Oholiab. These guys were gifted. Expert level at everything. They were anointed craftsmen, filled with the Spirit for good work. It would be impossible to separate their skill from the fact that they were also set apart for the work.

Apparently, without the Spirit of God inside ole Bezzy, there wouldn't have been any skill: "I have filled him with the Spirit of God, with ability and intelligence, with knowledge and all craftsmanship" (v. 3). Bezalel's intelligence, knowledge, and even his whittling skills were inherited from God himself.

Without God, Oholiab wouldn't have been an appointed leader either, not even if he'd read John C. Maxwell ten times a day. He needed the anointing of the Almighty to accomplish his specific work.

The Bible gives a list of the work they did. They built "the tent of meeting, and the ark of the testimony, and the mercy seat that is on it, and all the furnishings of the tent, the table and its utensils, and the pure lampstand with all its utensils, and the altar of incense, and the altar of burnt offering with all its utensils, and the basin and its stand, and the finely worked garments, the holy garments for Aaron the priest and the garments of his sons, for their service as priests, and the anointing oil and the fragrant incense for the Holy Place" (vv. 7–11).

Oholiab and Bezalel could do it all. They were like mega foremen or super general contractors. They were supernaturally empowered jacks-of-all-trades. How? Because the Almighty abided with them. "According to all that I have commanded you, they shall do," the Lord said (v. 11).

Notice the "all that I have commanded you" portion of the Exodus account. God was teaching Moses how his people must build patterns of life around the worship of himself. Woodwork was part of the plan, as were artistic design, goldsmithing, stonecutting, and all the other skills Bezalel had been given.

My favorite line in the whole passage might be this: "I have given to all able men ability, that they may make all that I have commanded" (v. 6).

Think about that for a moment.

God has given to all able men who serve him a measure of ability. They can do *work*, and they can do it because the Lord has given them ability. This is so much truer for Christian men than it is for other men.

And why does God give able-bodied men ability? *That they might do the work he has set for them to do.*

This truth makes me think of this awesome passage from the New Testament:

> We [Christians] are [God's] workmanship, created in Christ Jesus for good works, which God prepared beforehand, that we should walk in them. (Eph. 2:10)

In other words, God forged you, Christian man, into a custom tool because he had a whole truckload of works that he wanted human hands to accomplish.

Talk about finding significance in your work! Talk about finding meaning in any job. Talk about a calling!

RESURRECTED WORK

The Christian man is anointed for all his tasks. The skills and talents of a Christian man are automatically infused with God's power. We can and should improve our skill sets, but even if we don't, we're ahead of other men just because of our divine advantage.

Even so, it's possible for an anointed man to serve the Lord at a higher or lower capacity. Our anointing doesn't get called on if we're using our skills to, say, undercut a coworker or sabotage a boss. God isn't going to elevate your abilities if you're using them for purposes outside his will. Our motives are important too. When our motive is to hurt, tear down, or commit sin, those will not be anointed moments, though we remain anointed people.

What we want to produce is work that is resurrected. Rejuvenated. Empowered by God on high.

That means we have to follow through with the anointing. Remember, to be anointed means to be set apart for a holy purpose. Since we've been anointed as Christians, we cooperate with God's intention by realizing that we too are set apart for his service.

When I stood in that boardroom and cried out to God to do his work and bring his wisdom, I was cooperating with his anointing. I was lifting up myself and my abilities so he could maybe do a big thing. Which he did.

You can do that too. When you're on the job (or anywhere), intentionally offer your skills, talents, effort, and time to God as his skilled laborer.

When your motivation in work is to participate in giving glory to God—to see him manifested throughout the day—anointing flows. It supercharges all your work. Every task. Every meeting. Every confrontation. You'll begin to see that all things are already his. You're working with him with the tools he gave you.

When your will aligns with his will, your anointing is activated to fulfill God's purpose. That's when your work becomes resurrected.

That's when God might just do a big thing in and through you.

And he might do it so often that it becomes something you expect. Now, that's something that might make a job worth getting up for in the morning.

Daily Prayer

Lord, you are my rock. I believe there is not a thing I have to do that you could not teach me, if I ask.

You have anointed my head with oil (see Ps. 23:5). You have set me apart for good works (see Eph. 2:10).

Today I choose to act in accordance with the reality of Christ's anointing on me. I want to learn how to abide in your anointing. Give me new wisdom each day.

I want to do well by you, to be motivated by the right passions and the promises you've given me. Because of this, I choose to give you every one of my pressures during the day. This includes

_____.

As I abide in your love, may my work give glory to you. Forgive me if I've let this goal get out of focus.

I love you, and I'm excited to partner with you today.

In Christ, amen.

Chapter 5

THE FAITH AND THE MUSTARD SEED

Some trust in chariots and some in horses, but we
trust in the name of the LORD our God.

—Psalm 20:7

"Come," Jesus said (Matt. 14:29). One word. That's all he spoke.

But in that invitation, Peter had all the promise he needed to join Jesus on the water. He didn't need swimming lessons. He didn't need a pool floaty or water wings. He didn't even need to know how deep the water was beneath him. Peter simply needed to act on the invitation. So he stepped out of the boat and began floating on faith.

On those waves, the water was irrelevant. The wind was insignificant. The math of buoyancy didn't matter. All that mattered was Peter's relationship to faith. Moreover, his relationship with the Wave

Maker, through faith, made him capable of doing the impossible. In fact, this relationship was what allowed him to get out of the boat in the first place.

His friends told a different story. "It is a ghost!" they cried in terror (v. 26). They saw the situation—and Jesus—through their fear and the superstitions of sailors. Their minds were devoid of the divine.

But Simon Peter challenged what he saw and what his mind might've been telling him. When Christ said "Do not be afraid" (v. 27), it was good enough for Peter to test his faith. "Lord, if it is you," he said, "command me to come to you on the water" (v. 28).

He received his answer while the others waited inside the boat. He walked out, defying physics, and left the others behind in their unbelief. After a while, he sank, and the Lord caught him. Then together they walked on, continuing to do the impossible … through God's power.

The same invitation extends to you, brother. Once you have a vision for what a faith-filled situation can look like, step out. God will move the pieces, even commanding the water to catch each of your steps.

When we put our eyes on Jesus and our hope and faith in him, incredible things become possible. Yes, even at work. And even at work, when we take our eyes *off* Jesus and start trusting in our own abilities, the impossible becomes, well, impossible. We lose power and we go down.

In his job a Christian man has the tendency to trust in his own abilities. He's pretty good at a bunch of things related to the work and a bunch of things unrelated to the work. He's got experience and personal strengths that he brings to the job. Some Christian men are pretty darn impressive, when you get right down to it.

Yet we long to have God involved in our work. How can we find the balance?

TRUSTING IN ARMOR

Let's look first at a guy who got the balance all wrong. It's another great story from the Bible— the story of Saul, first king of Israel.

Saul was a man who was head and shoulders above the competition (see 1 Sam. 9:2). If there had been an MBA in that day, the guy would've had it. In fact, in the entire nation of Israel, no one was better credentialed than Saul to get the job done. He was immensely gifted, in the natural sense, for what he was called to do. He was made king, after all.

For a while, Saul walked in humility as king. He remembered that he had nothing that the Lord had not given to him. But at some point, Saul began to rest on his laurels. He began to believe his own press releases. He started trusting in his armor over the Almighty.

Let's look in on King Saul when he's in military and political checkmate—a perfect time to put faith in God (see 1 Sam. 17:1– 50). An army from Philistia had invaded Israel and was rampaging through the land. Saul mustered the Israelite army and marched out to meet the Philistines. The armies camped on opposite hillsides across a creek valley. Every day the Philistine champion—this huge warrior who stood more than nine feet tall—marched forward and challenged an Israelite champion to single combat.

Saul knew better than to march out there himself. He had good armor and weapons, so he could probably take a hit and land a blow or two. But Goliath had armor too, and his spear was basically a sharpened telephone pole. It would be over in seconds, and then Israel would be under foreign control.

If Saul had considered his heritage, then he would've remembered countless stories of God winning battles on this nation's behalf—armies and giants notwithstanding. But he'd long ago quit trusting in God, which left him with only the tools he'd been given.

He couldn't fight, and there were no Goliaths in the Israelite army, so he couldn't send anyone else out either. They could maybe refuse single combat and try to get the armies to join in battle, but with Goliath out there, could even the whole Israelite army win the field? So, day after day, the two armies stared at each other across the brook, and day after day, Israel did not send anyone out to meet the giant's challenge.

That's when a teenager was brought before Saul. This kid named David volunteered to fight Goliath, and he claimed he could beat him too. Saul prepared the lad to go into battle.

Now we might expect Saul, as king of God's chosen people, to have backed David up by exhorting him to pray and calling on him to fight in the power of the Lord. Instead, Saul gave David the king's own armor.

This was a mistake. Never fight any enemy of the faith with the same weapons the enemy is using. There is no fighting fire with fire in kingdom combat. There will always be someone bigger, faster, and better than you, humanly speaking.

Saul's wartime wares were a gift. The armor was fit for a king. The rich tunic, bronze helmet, and royal sword all rightfully belonged to him. They were possessions granted by God himself, items that came with his position and were meant to be used. I suspect Saul, fully clad in them, would've felt nearly invincible.

He might have forgotten this little fact, but Saul's armor and weapons were not the source of his strength as Israel's king. His strength and authority came from the Lord God, and the king related to God through faith. David and Saul were perfect opposites. Saul trusted in his armor, though he knew it wouldn't be enough. David trusted in God so much that armor was useless.

David knew that what would win the battle was faith, not armor or weapons. He understood that the sling and the Spirit cannot be separated.

But this was not true of the king. Despite watching David defeat the giant and save Israel, Saul continued to put his faith in what he possessed. Years later, in his final fight, he wore his armor into battle. It had been a long time since he'd had faith in the One who had provided him the position to even have the gear. To the end, he trusted in his own abilities and possessions, not in God. And eventually this mind-set killed him:

> The next day, when the Philistines came to strip the slain, they found Saul and his sons fallen on Mount Gilboa. And they stripped him and took his head

and his armor, and sent messengers throughout
the land of the Philistines to carry the good news
to their idols and to the people. And they put his
armor in the temple of their gods and fastened his
head in the temple of Dagon.... So Saul died for
his breach of faith. He broke faith with the LORD
in that he did not keep the command of the LORD.
(1 Chron. 10:8–10, 13)

Saul put all his faith in himself—in his armor and his own
strength—and this is what it got him. His faith in self was his undo-
ing. In a sense, his armor became his idol. His body was stripped
of the armor he'd trusted in. How ironic that his head and helmet
found their final resting place in the temple of his enemy.

In a sense, they'd been there all along.

A MAN AND HIS HANDS

When Christian men think about expressing their faith in the workplace, many of them imagine themselves not cussing (too much) on
the job, not stealing office supplies, not falsifying travel expenses,
not sleeping around, not slacking off on the job, and not stabbing
other workers in the back. You know, just basically being a "good
Christian."

None of those things have to do with faith. I mean, yes, when
you're walking with Christ, you won't be doing those things. But

good behavior is different from God-empowered behavior. Living morally might be a sign of faith, or it might just be something pretended for a time.

I'm also not describing that other way of thinking about having faith on the job, which says, "I'm going to use my skills to glorify God. And when I have enough faith to accomplish something amazing for the Lord, then everyone will acknowledge that only God could do something like that, and everyone will come to Jesus." Well, that would be nice, but more often than not, that attitude ends up condemning you. You think *you* have to manifest "enough faith," but you never can. So the big, amazing thing never happens, and the grand revival never begins.

What those approaches have in common is that they rely on the person, the Christian man, to provide the resources to make God-sized things happen. That was Saul's problem—Saul's *idolatry*—as he trusted in his armor, not the Almighty, to accomplish the things of God. And because you and I can't do the things for God we wish to do, we may feel condemned and like failures. That's definitely not what the Lord wants for us.

When a Christian man looks at his hands, meaning his abilities, he can't see them as the things that will make a difference in the world. When a man's hands can change the world is when they've become the instruments of God.

It's never the hands or the armor or the skill set of the man that is going to glorify God and draw people to him. It's the Spirit working through those things that will draw all people. Our skill sets are nothing if they're not given over to God's control. Without the Spirit doing the work, our hands labor in vain at every task (see Ps. 127:1).

If you want to find your calling in whatever job you have, then understand that every good thing you are and every good thing you bring to the job has been given to you by God. They can't do anything on their own. When you place them back under his authority and put your faith in him, that's when the power begins to flow.

WELL DONE, GOOD AND FAITHFUL SERVANT

We want to do our best in our jobs. We want to have pride (the good kind) and the feeling that we've given excellent work and earned an honest wage.

Am I saying here that hard work isn't important, because we're trusting God to elevate what we do? Not at all! But there is a difference between hard work as an end in itself and hard work in service of the Lord.

Jesus told a parable about a rich man who went on a journey and left his servants in charge of conducting business while he was gone (see Matt. 25:14–30). When he returned, he called the servants together so they could give a report about what they did with their talents (that's a unit of money). In the passage below, the rich man gave a response that every man would love to hear said about him:

> He who had received the five talents came forward,
> bringing five talents more, saying, "Master, you
> delivered to me five talents; here, I have made five
> talents more." His master said to him, "Well done,
> good and faithful servant. You have been faithful
> over a little; I will set you over much. Enter into the
> joy of your master." (vv. 20–21)

"Well done, good and faithful servant." Wow. It's like a statement of total approval laid across your entire life and personality. To hear that said about you … now, that would be an incentive.

That's one reason we work so hard on the job, as Christian men. Faithful, loyal, dedicated work is admirable and godly. It is definitely how we would expect a Christian man to work. But that's not the focus of faith-filled work.

Consider this: There is no such thing as hard work. There is no 110 percent.

I know that's a hard pill to swallow. When we come at work from a faith perspective, however, there is only work that is "well done" and work that isn't.

Many Christian men work hard in an attempt to keep the moral high ground and act like good Christians. Because, when we're working hard, at least we'll be seen as doing the right thing. But this is condemning because, if there's ever a time when we don't work hard, we feel that we'll miss out on that "Well done, good and faithful servant" from our Lord.

This is a mind game of Satan. For Christian men, our hard work—our backbreaking toil or our impressive résumés—is not the measure of a job well done. It's not about an eight-hour day going on twenty. It's not about a double master's degree going on a doctorate. It's not about putting in overtime instead of taking downtime. That's a trap, because if your sense of worth is wrapped up in earning merit, you're in for a long, sad career.

Now, working quietly, steadily, and diligently can indeed be a witness to unbelievers. Sometimes a workplace can be such that just having a positive attitude and not complaining all the time will make you stand out.

But you step into the big leagues when you offer yourself to God as his servant and see yourself as a vessel bringing the Holy Spirit to your jobsite. Apply your faith as David did when he walked out to face Goliath. Bring your confidence in Jesus to all the scenarios you encounter at work. Faith is always functional—perfect for everyday uses.

CHOOSING FAITH

Consider yourself as being set aside by God for a holy purpose at your job. Here's a great passage about this from the New Testament:

> In a great house there are not only vessels of gold
> and silver but also of wood and clay, some for
> honorable use, some for dishonorable. Therefore, if

anyone cleanses himself from what is dishonorable,
he will be a vessel for honorable use, set apart as
holy, useful to the master of the house, ready for
every good work. (2 Tim. 2:20–21)

You and I are vessels in God's house, and we have been designated for honorable use. We're there to hold ripe fruit or riches or wine for the king. We're not chamber pots! Some of us are vessels of gold and silver, used for fancy banquets. Others of us are vessels of wood and clay, made for more workaday, sensible tasks. But all of us have been both made and placed by the Master of the great house. We're to be available, and we're to be here for his purposes, not our own agendas. We are here at all—and we are *where* we are—because he wants us to be "ready for every good work."

How's that for a calling?

What did Paul mean when he talked about cleansing ourselves from what is dishonorable? He meant a few things, including putting away sins we know we need to get rid of. But he also meant that we should stop filling our work lives with neutral or even good things that aren't the highest expression of what God has called us to be. For Christian men working a job, it means we need to put away all our human-level junk and mind games and instead concentrate on offering ourselves to him as set-apart vessels "ready for every good work."

The Master of the house has given you a home and purpose. You are invited to take part in the Almighty's work in the world. To be ready for good and honorable work means to be free of lesser purposes. So, then, the prudent man looks at the vessel of his heart and what it can hold. He cleans out every dishonor, starting with his attitude.

For the typical man, it is the little things that keep him from bringing faith to the job effectively. Little things that aren't wrong necessarily but that don't keep our eyes on the goal. The small habits—like how we evaluate other people's work or how quickly we leave when the clock hits 5:00 p.m. or the distractions we give ourselves when we don't enjoy the task at hand—are what get in the way of meaningful work. Momentary delights siphon the opportunity for sanctification to bring out more godly desires.

Maybe you can see in this passage that the vessel actually has the choice to be set apart for honorable use. The choice is based on whether the Christian man "cleanses himself from what is dishonorable."

One way we do this is by choosing to bring God into our work and to offer ourselves and our skill sets for his purposes.

Years ago, when my business had not been around for long, I received an amazing (and, frankly, terrifying) opportunity. The president of a luxury cabinet line wanted me to help create the marketing branding for a new product. This was the big time. Some of their custom offerings went for several hundred dollars per square foot, and the CEO of Twitter had used them and knew the owner.

So how was I supposed to offer any value? I knew I had a lot of skills I could bring into the situation, and I wanted to be seen as this whiz kid who thought of the best approach and angles. But I also wanted to be a vessel for noble purposes.

So I prayed before the first meeting. Even so, I found their factory large and intimidating. There were employees everywhere. There was so much at stake with the work I might be doing. Once more, I was tempted to rest on my skill set. That, or run away very quickly.

But I reminded myself that opportunity and faith go hand in hand. The Lord had provided this opportunity. My job was simply to step into it and believe he would do the rest.

This is what I want you to remember for this chapter: when God provides the opportunity, he will provide what's needed to accomplish the tasks before you.

In the meeting I learned that my tasks would be to brand the product line, develop a name that could compete in the market, and create their online strategy for it. While I'd done similar things, this was the first time I would do it at this scale. I should've been quivering in my loafers, but I remembered that God would provide whatever I needed—ideas, analysis, etc.—to do this job in a way that was anointed and that glorified him.

Back at my office, I prayed again, committing it all to him and offering myself as his servant … and then I stepped confidently into the creative process. At every phase I gave the job prayerfully to the Lord. It was incredible to know that he was walking beside me in it. I stayed alert to those moments when I felt him inspiring me.

He didn't let me down. The client loved everything I did, and the launch went off without a hitch.

Sometime after the product was launched, I received a call from the president of the company. He was happy to report that they had broken their initial sales goal and were well into seven-figure revenue. He was elated. I was relieved. But God was glorified through the work I did.

When God provides the opportunity, he provides what you need to meet it in a way that honors him.

That should give you peace as you think about your job. No matter how you landed this work, God has brought you to it. He has given you the opportunity, and he has a large set of works he'd like to accomplish through you. If you're a vessel for noble purposes and you're ready for his use, it's time to get to work.

IMMANUEL AT THE OFFICE

At Christmastime we hear the word *Immanuel* a lot. It means "God with us," and it's what happened when the Son of God entered humanity in the form of baby Jesus. God left heaven and came to be with us.

There's a limited sense in which that's our job, too, as Christian men on the work site or in the office or at the store or in the classroom. We are human vessels carrying the Spirit of God and walking among humanity.

Just as Jesus did the works of his Father during his earthly ministry (see John 4:34), so we have works that the Father wants to accomplish through us in our jobs. Jesus brought the mind, heart, wisdom, and love of God to bear on every situation he encountered. That's our task as well.

Here are some sample workplace scenarios and a starter idea for how you might bring faith in God—not faith in your skills or your armor—to each one:

- You're asked to do a task you really don't want to do. You need faith to attack it and accomplish it well.
- Your job takes place in a spiritually dark work environment. It needs your faith that it can be changed. How should it change? Pray about it.
- You're handed a project you don't know how to execute. You need faith that the Holy Spirit will endow you with wisdom. When you ask, he will provide—every time.
- You have an antagonist at your job. This person hates you seemingly for no reason. As Paul said, you should no longer "regard [that person] according to the flesh" (2 Cor. 5:16). It takes faith to see the potential that God has placed in him or her. Ask God exactly what that person's potential is—then draw it out of him or her.
- You are given a subordinate who is a slow learner. You need faith to ask for wisdom to teach him or her. That person is under your care. For now, you're the Christ that person knows.
- You have a boss who is unreasonable. You need faith to lead those who are up the ladder from

you as well as those who are down the ladder from you. Part of being a kingdom player is not abiding by the world's system of role-based leadership.

- You're asked to be dishonest. It takes faith to believe that God weighs the scales. We must trust him.

Every day you are faced with situations that need faith if you are to be a vessel for noble purposes. Every day you have the opportunity—and sometimes the desperate need—to call out to God in faith about how to respond.

In your workplace, look for a few areas that need to change for the good. Identify what should change and why. Imagine and meditate on what the situation might look like if God were to touch it. Ask the Lord for specifics. As you can guess, he likely has something in mind.

Your workplace may be where God has brought one or more people who need to know Jesus, and he may have put you there because that's one of the noble uses he has for you. Perhaps you're there to show compassion or God's concern for the oppressed. Perhaps you're there to bring joy into a sad or toxic environment. Perhaps you're there to speak out against corruption.

Once you have a vision for what that situation might look like if God were brought into it, act on it. Step forward in faith boldly. If God has given the opportunity, he'll provide the means. He will move the pieces, even commanding the water to bear you up as you move toward his purpose.

When you're trusting not in your armor but in the Almighty and when you're offering your skill set to him for his goals, you'll be like an Immanuel in the workplace. When you're standing in front of all the executives or you're in some other important situation, you'll see yourself as dependent on God to do the work that needs to be done. You'll find yourself walking on the water because of God's power, realizing even as you do it that there's no way you could do this on your own.

Daily Prayer

Father, without you I can do no good thing. So, before I give you my labor, I want to give you my love.

I am so thankful for the work you've given me. Help me not place my faith in my gifting over the gift of your Son. I am aware of my positional inheritance. I won't live in false humility about the things you've asked me to steward.

Help me also work with gratitude, growing in the knowledge of you. Expand my heart. Make me into an honorable vessel, set apart for holy work.

Thank you for giving me a lifetime of opportunity. I give myself to you fully to make you known and to be known by you. I want nothing except you—no worldly progress that is without your guidance and support.

Strengthen me as I go about this day. I invite you into all of it.

In Christ, amen.

Chapter 6

THE FIRE AND
THE BONES

*If I say, "I will not mention him, or speak any
more in his name," there is in my heart as it were
a burning fire shut up in my bones, and I am
weary with holding it in, and I cannot.*

—Jeremiah 20:9

Nine spider bites dotted my back like some kind of throbbing constellation. Each one was a painful reminder that my circumstances needed to change. I was living in an oil tank on my parents' farm. A small tank not being used to store oil, thankfully. And though this was my new home, it was not the first time I had woken up bitten. But this morning certainly hurt the worst.

The tank sat sixty feet behind the barn, just beyond the family's trash burn pile. It wasn't exactly a bachelor pad, but it gave me a little more elbow room than I'd had in the crowded situation with my siblings. Not having to share a bed with three other brothers was one of the oil tank's top amenities. The black widow spiders—and their less poisonous cousins—were not.

The round industrial oil drum was hot and leaky, and moisture from the ground constantly soaked through the perforated metal floor. During the summer the temperature inside was well into the triple digits. But for a boy of fifteen, it might as well have been a penthouse.

I had scrubbed the oil on the walls with a mixture of soap and paint thinner, and the grime had eventually given way. There was no electricity in it. I was, however, able to drag an extension cord from the back of the barn into that rusty tank for some lights hung near the top. With these lights, an old abandoned love seat, and a small hand-me-down school desk, I had nearly everything I required to start something new.

All I needed was a computer.

My plan was to start practicing graphic design, something I knew little about. But it appealed to me, and I wanted to create a means to new opportunity. After school each day, I worked odd jobs to save money toward the purchase of a computer.

At last the opportunity to buy came during a late-night super sale at a local retailer. You had to get one of the discount vouchers they were handing out and use it to take advantage of the special price.

But when I arrived, my hopes were smashed. Apparently I wasn't the only person who wanted a computer on the cheap. More than

250 people were already in line ahead of me, starting right at the doors, which hadn't yet reopened for the event.

I was not about to give up on my dream. I believed that God had set a career in technology before me, and I sensed I needed to take initiative to punch through to that future. So I started campaigning.

With my younger brother holding my place, I moved toward the front of the line, and I soon found one of my friends right near the earliest arrivers. I explained to him my pressing need for a new computer, and he got to work.

It turned out that he knew several people in line around him. He began to ask them whether they would be willing to give up their discount vouchers, because having one of those was the only way I would be able to pay for my dream. To my amazement, someone eventually agreed to give me their voucher. If you'd seen my reaction, you would've thought I had won the lottery. And though I had taken charge, God was leading the way.

I spent the remainder of my high school years at that computer, dutifully practicing my design and programming skills in the oil tank. I got bit by various arachnids. Once, I even got bit by a mantis that I'm pretty sure hadn't been praying. Sometimes water soaked up from the ground onto my power cord, threatening to kill my dream (and me).

If someone had seen me there—this poor kid from East Texas living in a barrel—that person might've thought my prospects were low.

But every time I acted with what I did have, the Lord met me in my work. He handed me new opportunities to partner with local ministries and share creative thinking with people who needed it.

God had a whole plan for me that was so much better than I could've dreamed.

A WORD ABOUT EMOTIONALITY

I was extremely excited when I got that discount voucher. Overjoyed. It seemed like a world of promise had been handed to me in that little sheet of perforated paper. But when I went home and started the long process of learning new skills, the emotion soon faded, and commitment took its place.

That's the way it is for Christian men in their careers as well.

When men think about their jobs, the idea of emotion doesn't often come up. Even if they really like their work, they don't usually get emotional about it. In the end, even a good job is, on some level, just a job. It's the thing you do week in and week out to pay the bills.

But I've found that when I start talking to some Christian men about serving God on the job, all of a sudden, emotionality enters the conversation. They start wondering whether they feel hyped or stoked enough to serve God at work. Many of them don't feel hyped enough, which can make them feel condemned. They try to connect the workplace with the emotional high they associate with weekend worship, and if they don't feel the same emotions, they can start to wonder whether they're just not called by God to serve him at work—or even whether they're called at all.

Whatever level of heightened emotionality we may experience in church worship, we need to be sure we're not expecting to feel like that when we clock in at the plant. In some jobs a steady hand is required—emotions running wild at work might even be dangerous.

The picture of a Christian man serving God at work is not of a guy doing leaping chest bumps and high fives. There *is* great purpose and fulfillment to be found by serving God on a job, and that does bring a deep sense (or emotion) of peace, but you can leave your megaphone at home.

This brings up a related subject. You've heard the saying "He's so heavenly minded that he's of no earthly good." I've seen that happen in the workplace. Guys who pepper their language with "Hallelujah" and offer to pray with non-Christian coworkers in the hallways and make sure everyone hears them listening to Christian music … but don't do their jobs well.

I encourage men to keep their spiritual eyes open and their spiritual ears to the ground to detect opportunities to bring light into dark lives at work. That's what this book is about! However, they've been hired to do a job. If they do it well and bring honor and support to the boss and the company and the customer and if their deadlines allow it, then yes, there might be openings to talk about faith. That's how you earn the right to speak to workers on the job.

But if they're neglecting their actual job in order to "talk Jesus" and if they don't hit their deadlines or work with excellence or do all the other things that are expected of them, they're not honoring the Lord or working for their earthly boss as unto the Lord (see Col. 3:23).

In that case, they should be fired.

Now, before you think this is too harsh, let's be clear: there is absolutely nothing wrong with praying for people at work, listening to worship on the factory floor, or asking the Lord for wisdom before your meetings.

But if you think this "church work" is the type of energy you need to have in order to be involved in kingdom building on the job, you're fooling yourself. The world desperately needs answers. They want to know whether the God-life has real influence and brings deliverance and changes one's outlook during the day. If our affections are shown only for our Sunday stint, then we've separated our calling from our career.

Jesus did not separate the nail and cross from the hand between them. Neither do we separate our resolve to seek the Spirit from what he wants to accomplish through us during the day. And that's the best part. This kind of resolve will actually produce the passion God wants to develop within you for the work at hand.

What I can promise you is that the more you learn how to join God's great task—not only at work but also in all areas of your life—the more you'll find that passion is growing in you. A measure of excitement will rise in you as you clock in, because you can't wait to see what God is going to do today in the lives around you.

A FIRE IN THE BONES

What do you get fired up about? What kinds of things can get you up on a Saturday morning or keep you burning the midnight oil? What are your personal passion projects?

Every man is passionate about at least one thing. His kids, maybe, or his favorite NFL team. Politics, mountain biking, smartphones, or working in the wood shop. The church softball league, fast computers, voting, or the Indianapolis 500. Christian men have plenty of passion. Even when we're sick or discouraged and at our lowest, some things will get a rise out of us, no matter what.

Of course, not everything generates as much enthusiasm in us as our favorite pastimes. Doing our taxes, for example (sorry if you love doing taxes!), taking out the trash, or spending the day with certain extended-family members.

But when it comes to an object of our passion, it's as if *a fire rises in our bones*, and we engage the challenge wholeheartedly. Those words come from this verse in the Old Testament:

> If I say, "I will not mention him, or speak any more in his name," there is in my heart as it were *a burning fire shut up in my bones*, and I am weary with holding it in, and I cannot. (Jer. 20:9)

The prophet Jeremiah was tired of preaching to God's people that doom and destruction were coming. The people were mocking him and telling him to shut up (see v. 8). Who needed that? But when he thought about going silent and squelching God's messages, he felt as if he would explode—with fire.

He couldn't sit still. He couldn't remain quiet. The work God had called him to was urgent. It was an emergency message that could spell life or death for God's people. How could he not be up and about that work? How could he shut himself in his house and let the disaster come on them when there was the possibility that even one more family would be saved?

Seven centuries later, another man of God wrestled with fire in his bones. The Apostle Paul was consumed with the task of spreading the gospel and raising up disciples. This is the calling all Christians have been given, and Paul felt the urgency of it in his very veins. The fire in Paul's bones came as he traveled around warning everyone and teaching everyone with all wisdom that we may present everyone mature in Christ. "For this I toil, struggling with all his energy that he powerfully works within me" (Col. 1:28–29).

If you close your eyes, you can almost see Paul's pen quivering. As he wrote, he no doubt recounted the times when he had experienced the Lord working through him. What powerful, conquering energy ran through his veins! Can you imagine it? The Spirit coursed through his body so strongly, so inexplicably, that the energy had to be physically struggled with.

It's hard to convey in English the power words Paul used in this one sentence, but I'm going to try to do so in a personal translation:

> For this purpose (spreading the gospel and teaching disciples), I wear myself completely out, fighting mightily in agony with the energy that empowers me with explosive might.

We get our English words *agony, energy,* and *dynamite* from forms of Greek words used in this sentence. Paul used words related to *energy* twice here, just to show how "energetically energized" God's dynamite in his body had made him.

No wonder he struggled to contain it! No wonder he couldn't sit still. That explosive energy produced godly toil that brought irrevocable damage to the kingdom of darkness. And all that while Paul was locked in prison! What an unfair advantage we have over Paul's circumstances.

God is doing a big thing in the world. Accomplishing a great task. The works that Jesus did, God's Spirit is still doing—only now he does them in partnership with Christians (see John 14:12). The things Jesus was about, God is still about. The situations that drew his attention then draw his attention now. The works that Jesus said his Father was always doing (see v. 10) are the works he's still doing today.

Jesus called for more workers to join him in the great harvest of God (see Matt. 9:37–38). Guess what, my brother? That's you and me!

What are the works of God? What does it mean to join him in the work of harvesting? Here's what Jesus said his mission was:

> [Jesus] came to Nazareth, where he had been brought up. And as was his custom, he went to the synagogue on the Sabbath day, and he stood up to read. And the scroll of the prophet Isaiah was given

to him. He unrolled the scroll and found the place
where it was written,

> "The Spirit of the Lord is upon me,
>> because he has anointed me
>> to proclaim good news to the poor.
> He has sent me to proclaim liberty to the captives
>> and recovering of sight to the blind,
>> to set at liberty those who are oppressed,
> to proclaim the year of the Lord's favor."

And he rolled up the scroll and gave it back to
the attendant and sat down. And the eyes of all in
the synagogue were fixed on him. And he began to
say to them, "Today this Scripture has been fulfilled
in your hearing." (Luke 4:16–21)

Jesus took as his mission the same mission God has always had:

1. Proclaim good news to the poor.
2. Proclaim liberty to the captives.
3. Bring recovery of sight to the blind.
4. Liberate those who are oppressed.
5. Proclaim the year of the Lord's favor.

That's a big work. It's unending, so long as the earth persists.
And it's beautifully applicable to every situation and age.

THE PRACTICAL SIDE OF ANOINTING

In chapter 4 we said anointing is a natural skill elevated by the Spirit of God to accomplish God's purposes. That's step one. Now let's go to step two, the practical application of anointing. In other words, the way we tune in to the energetic energy God has for kingdom building.

When Jesus sent his twelve disciples out two by two (see Mark 6:7–13; Luke 9:1–6), he gave them his power and authority. He basically deputized them—or we could say he *anointed* them—to be his representatives and to carry out his mission in six places at once. They knew the five elements of his task (proclaim good news to the poor, etc.), and they sought opportunities to implement those elements wherever they went. His supernatural power went with them, and they found they were suddenly capable of feats of healing and spiritual warfare.

Why? Because they had been (1) sent out by Christ (2) as his servants and ambassadors (3) to pursue the great mission that Jesus himself was on earth to pursue and (4) the power and authority of the Almighty went with them.

They became bearers of God's mission and power. They became the direct applicators of God's intent in the world—of his will being done on earth as it is in heaven (see Matt. 6:10).

This is how anointing happens practically: when we place ourselves in service to God and pursue the great task he is still pursuing, he uses us. This is what it means to offer our skills and selves to God as "instruments for righteousness" (Rom. 6:13). Jesus himself was the hands and feet of God the Father, and we perform the same purpose for Jesus.

This isn't about being emotionally pumped, but come on—doesn't that get a rise out of you, just a bit? You don't have to be clergy to get excited about becoming the guy whose job it is to carry God's power and to pursue the mission he's always had.

When we present ourselves for God's purposes and his Spirit abides in us, we are deputized by Jesus in the same way the Twelve were. We are likewise (1) sent out by Christ (2) as his servants and ambassadors (3) to pursue the great mission that Jesus himself was on earth to pursue, and therefore, we can expect that (4) the power and authority of the Almighty goes with us.

So get excited. Christ has come. His work is finished. The veil between labor and love is torn. Now there is no separation between the presence of God and the indwelling of his power within you. You are set in the saddle. The reins of righteous living are in your hands. Through resurrection your work is made new in his life. You have authority over dead work—for Christ and King.

JESUS' MISSION ... AT YOUR JOB

But how do you take the mission Jesus had as he walked along the dusty desert paths of Israel and apply it to corporate America or wherever your job takes place? How do you abide in the calling of Christ? Let's take a closer look at his missional work.

Here's the list again, taken from Luke 4:

1. Proclaim good news to the poor.
2. Proclaim liberty to the captives.
3. Bring recovery of sight to the blind.
4. Liberate those who are oppressed.
5. Proclaim the year of the Lord's favor.

These are the five fruits of calling. If these kinds of things are happening around you, then the fire and passion of God are working through you and you're building the kingdom.

Let's start with number one: good news.

First, how can you proclaim good news to the poor when you're at work? The good news Jesus was referring to is that salvation has been freely offered to all, not just to those the world considers important. God's concern is for every person, no matter how small. Who at your job needs to know that God has not forgotten him or her? Which coworker could use the relief of God's love and forgiveness? The Lord will provide opportunities to share his good news, so be watching for them.

Second, how can you proclaim liberty to the captives at your jobsite? God's heart inclines most to those who are oppressed, abused, imprisoned, threatened, and crushed. Cruel treatment of the weak and innocent is what keeps the fire of God's anger stoked. Who is harassed and held captive, in any sense, at your place of work? God reaches out with furious love to innocents who are harmed. Why not be the hands that fully extend his relief to them?

Third, how can you bring recovery of sight to the blind at work? This refers to all sorts of healing and relief for those who are afflicted. Jesus brought physical healing, and he brought healing to the inner person. He brought light to those who were blind, physically or spiritually. Who is blind, in any sense, where you work? Who needs light? Who needs healing or encouragement? Pray for eyes to see these needs, and then look around.

Fourth, how can you set at liberty those who are oppressed when you're at work? Really, what is the condition of spiritual lostness but captivity of the Devil? Jesus came to proclaim the kingdom of God, and that is our task too, no matter our jobs. You have your own style of doing this, and different situations and people require different approaches. But let's always keep in mind that the greatest way to bring relief to the hurting is to lead people to Jesus.

Finally, how can you proclaim the year of the Lord's favor on the job? From the moment Jesus sent the Holy Spirit to live in believers (see Acts 2), we have entered the year of the Lord's favor. God has thrown open the gates of heaven and invited everyone in. But the gates won't remain parted forever. Who knows when this limited-time offer will be ended? The good news is that everyone has been invited. The urgency is that the doors may even now be swinging shut. Who at your workplace needs to hear that God wants them to enter his gates?

These five fruits of calling can be applied to any job or life situation. This is your ministry and your calling.

Jesus said, "Whoever believes in me will do the works I have been doing, and they will do even greater things than these" (John

14:12 NIV). This wasn't rhetoric. He was not holding a pep rally for students of a seminary. He made a promise: you will do the same work as he did.

GIVE ME THIS MOUNTAIN

Caleb in the Old Testament was a Rambo in the Spirit, a man who loved mission impossible. When God had delivered his people from Egypt and led them to the edge of the Promised Land, Caleb was one of the twelve Jewish men chosen to spy out the land.

When the twelve returned to Moses and the children of Israel, ten of the spies gave a bad report about the inhabitants of the land. "They're too big, too mighty, and too many," they said. They had little confidence in what their soldiers could do against the hordes of pagans, not least against the giants called Anakim, the ancestors of Goliath (see Num. 13). The report of the ten spies caused the courage of the people of God to fail (see 14:1–4).

Caleb and Joshua jumped up and tried to get the people to trust in God, who had not too long before conquered Pharaoh's mighty army. But the people picked up rocks to stone Caleb and Joshua to death, and they would've succeeded had God not personally intervened (see vv. 6–10).

God punished the children of Israel, and a generation later, when they again stood on the brink of the Promised Land, Caleb and Joshua were living, but no one remained of all the adults who had doubted God after the spies' report. This time Israel did not doubt

God, and God led his people in a great conquest of the land he had given as their inheritance. Even the Anakim were overthrown (but, as we'll see, not completely destroyed).

Forty-five years after Caleb and the spies had done their recon run, the Promised Land belonged to the Jewish people. There were pockets of pagan resistance, but all the tribes of Israel were in their allotted places. The last item to be tended to was the place where Caleb, now eighty-five, would settle.

Perhaps not surprisingly, Caleb said he wanted to settle in Hebron, which was where the Anakim had lived.

This is one of my favorite stories from the Bible:

> The people of Judah came to Joshua at Gilgal. And Caleb the son of Jephunneh the Kenizzite said to him … "I was forty years old when Moses … sent me … to spy out the land.… Moses swore on that day, saying, 'Surely the land on which your foot has trodden shall be an inheritance for you and your children forever, because you have wholly followed the LORD my God.' And now, behold, the LORD has kept me alive, just as he said, these forty-five years since the time that the LORD spoke this word to Moses, while Israel walked in the wilderness. And now, behold, I am this day eighty-five years old. I am still as strong today as I was in the day that Moses sent me; my strength now is as my strength was then, for war and for going and coming. So

now *give me this hill country* of which the LORD
spoke on that day, for you heard on that day how
the Anakim were there, with great fortified cities. It
may be that the LORD will be with me, and I shall
drive them out just as the LORD said."

Then Joshua blessed him, and he gave Hebron
to Caleb ... for an inheritance. (Josh. 14:6–13)

"Give me this hill country," Caleb said (v. 12). Some other trans-
lations read, "Give me this mountain" (KJV).

Age and time did not bother Caleb. Who cared that he was
eighty-five? *He* didn't. He was still as strong as in the day Moses sent
him out as a spy. "My strength now is as my strength was then, for
war and for going and coming" (v. 11). As my father, the marine,
might say, "Oorah!"

That's how the man of God can be when he knows what has
been promised to him by the Lord. Caleb walked in the full assurance that what God had promised, God would bring to pass. When
you know what reward is coming to you, you don't mind taking
initiative to step boldly toward it.

Since Caleb had been promised the ground his feet had walked
on and since those feet had walked throughout the land, he might've
been able to pick any region he wanted. He selected Hebron—the
seat of fearsome giant warriors even then—as the place where he
would watch God bring about his promise.

The Bible tells how Caleb and his men "drove out from there the
three sons of Anak, Sheshai and Ahiman and Talmai, the descendants

of Anak" (Josh. 15:14). Giants were overthrown by a man who believed what God had said.

I love the picture of eighty-five-year-old Caleb standing before eighty-something-year-old Joshua, saying, "I am still as strong today as I was in the day Moses sent me out as a spy. So *give me that mountain* and watch God kick some very large backsides."

My friend, God has given you a plot of land as well, spiritually speaking. The inheritance God has given you is a land whose boundaries encompass your place of work (and beyond). It is a place where the relief, healing, hope, light, and liberty of the Lord reach those who are suffering and oppressed.

You are like Caleb on the verge of taking on the Anakim: you already know what the outcome is going to be, even though it hasn't happened yet. You are like the disciples sent out by Jesus with his power and authority: you will begin to see God's power working through you.

You have been strategically moved into your place of labor. Your inheritance—composed of people who can come to enjoy the liberty of the Lord's favor—stands in front of you. The way may be blocked by giants, but that doesn't matter because you have the promise and authority of almighty God.

This is your calling. This is what you are working toward and fighting against. The land you're taking is already yours. Get rid of the insecurity of whether this calling belongs to you or whether it will have any impact.

When I walk into any job or consulting situation, I assume that the decisions I make and advice I give will cause change. Why?

Because I'm so smart and experienced? No. It's because I know that I have been anointed and sent by God to bring his power into these situations. Because of who I am in Christ, I know that what I say will have a real effect on the room.

The land is yours and the battle is won. You still need to gather your men and take the enemy strongholds, of course. You still have to trust God as you take initiative to move toward what he's promised. But now you have good reason for the fire in your bones. Now you can move forward with confidence.

Years after I got that computer and took it back to the oil tank to learn new skills, I went through a time when the way to that promised future seemed blocked. I took a job at a church, thinking a detour into ministry might be what God had in mind for me for a while. But my heart was still set on what God had been teaching me in the tank.

Imagine my surprise—but not really—when, just a few days after starting at the church, one of the senior pastors came up to me and said, "We need someone who's media savvy and has an eye for design. Do you know anyone?"

Daily Prayer

Father God, light a fire in my bones. Consume me completely with holy initiative.

I desire to be like you. So I thank you for first taking initiative with me.

Help me, please, to take initiative in kingdom work too. Forgive me if I've seen my work as unworthy of your call.

Show me instead, today and in the future, how to wrestle with the energy you have put inside me until it produces a blessing—for me, for my family, and, ultimately, for my faith in you.

I want you to father me. So reveal to me the lies that inhibit godly ambition.

Show me what to pursue as I pursue you. I take you at your word and trust that you will stoke the embers of my life until I am full of pure fire for the life you want me to live and the work you want me to do.

I'm looking forward to it.

In Christ, amen.

Chapter 7

THE PLAN AND
THE PURPOSE

*The thief comes only to steal and kill and destroy. I came
that they may have life and have it abundantly.*

—John 10:10

I started a forest fire once.

Whenever planting season comes around in East Texas, it's best
to burn away all the weeds and brush so new vegetation will have
room to grow. You do this by creating a perimeter around the plot
of land where you are going to plant, and then you start a series of
controlled fires to clear out the garden. It's called brush burning.

If everything goes according to plan, the previous year's deadfall
is eliminated and nitrogen is put back into the soil. This creates the
best possible soil for new plant life to take root in.

Before we proceed in the story, just know that before I started this particularly memorable brush burning, I did take precautions. My family had a freshwater well two acres away from the garden I was preparing. I brought water from that well and soaked a three-foot border around the entire piece of land where we intended to plant food. I soaked the grass not one time, not two times, but *three times*.

You would think this would be enough. I definitely did.

However, each time I passed a certain corner of the garden, I felt a tug in my heart, as if maybe I hadn't tended to that spot adequately. The feeling annoyed me. I'd done my due diligence, after all. The grass was wet—drenched, even. I had also chosen a biblical number of times to make my watery moat.

But the internal nudge persisted. Yet I denied it.

With a match, I threw caution to the wind and lit the tinder in the center of the area to be burned.

Let's just say I learned many lessons that day.

When you're eighteen, the finer details of fire can escape you. In this case, they escaped me, the garden, my wet perimeter, *and* the nearby road to the highway. The wind almost instantly engulfed the entire garden in flames.

At first it seemed that the flames were contained within the perimeter of soaked grass. This pleased me despite the surprising flame I'd set. I was master of the elements. My gut feeling had obviously been wrong—easy enough to confuse in the Texas heat.

But after a few minutes, and to my horror, the flames broke out of their barrier—exactly in the corner where my lack of peace had persisted. The wind moved the fifteen-foot flames faster than I could run. To make matters worse, no hose was nearby.

Once the flames were free of my perimeter, the fire was unstoppable. The entire back pasture caught on fire, as did my neighbor's land. (He was, ironically, a firefighter.) Frantically I called 911 and explained the situation. No fewer than six fire trucks came to the rescue. Which was a good call, because by the time they arrived, the forest behind our property had caught fire as well.

The fire burned for two days. Thankfully no one was hurt and no property was destroyed. But that was due only to the heroic efforts of the firemen who fought the fire and used bulldozers to create a berm around the surrounding woods. Without them, the situation would have been much worse.

After the fire was under control, I explained what had happened to one of the firemen. He laughed as if he saw this same thing play out every Wednesday. He explained that the flames had found their way *under* the grass. Somehow the fire had burrowed underneath my perimeter.

The Holy Spirit had known this would happen, of course, and had tried to warn me. But I hadn't been interested in those details at the moment. I had just wanted to get the job done.

That was the day I learned the value of listening to the Lord while I worked.

WHAT'S THE POINT?

"What am I working toward?" Every man wants to know the purpose for his labor.

The men who discovered it did so by finding the path the Lord was on. Then they followed him.

Scripture says that God makes mountains low and valleys high (see Isa. 40:4), meaning that all you have to do is walk the path in front of you, seeking the Lord at each turn. He does the hard work of path making for you. Recall Romans 8:28: "We know that for those who love God all things work together for good, for those who are called according to his purpose."

All around you, the Spirit of God is at work in unseen ways. Part of his work is to meticulously orchestrate all things for your good. This includes the things that don't match your expectations. This includes fires that get out of hand. This includes the fallouts of finance and career. This includes the unknown. For those who love him, *all things* means "all things."

If you want to find God's purpose for you, you need to pursue it. Here's a great question to find out what God is doing with you now: "Lord, are you pruning me or planting me?"

That question will lead you to the discovery of what people, projects, and plans are being arranged so you can be about the real work of the kingdom.

ARE YOU BEING PRUNED?

Dead plants don't grow, and gardeners don't bother pruning them. But living plants can be helped toward greater fruitfulness through a prudent application of the shears. Still, any sort of cutting can hurt. "The Lord disciplines the one he loves, and chastises every son whom he receives" (Heb. 12:6).

Consider also the words of Jesus:

> Every branch in me that does not bear fruit he takes away, and every branch that does bear fruit he prunes, that it may bear more fruit. Already you are clean because of the word that I have spoken to you. Abide in me, and I in you. As the branch cannot bear fruit by itself, unless it abides in the vine, neither can you, unless you abide in me. I am the vine; you are the branches. Whoever abides in me and I in him, he it is that bears much fruit, for apart from me you can do nothing. If anyone does not abide in me he is thrown away like a branch and withers; and the branches are gathered, thrown into the fire, and burned. (John 15:2–6)

Our Father graciously removes the moss- and fungus-infected branches from our lives. He weeds out the things that don't support good fruit. Therefore, we have no reason to be afraid of the Spirit's shears. He cuts only what kills us. You and I can willingly participate in the pruning.

Many times, pruning comes in the form of a person. People who prune you will bring something to the table that you do not, which is one reason they bother you so much. Depending on how much pruning you need in an area, you may even get more than one such individual at once. This person's personality, approach to work, or the way he or she does things will likely be abrasive. This is for your benefit, and you can believe that the Lord is working things together for your good behind the scenes.

If you remain humble and in a posture of gratitude, you can begin to let the good Gardener do his work in your life. He will use the abrasive person to cut off the dead branches that prevent you from seeing the sun.

You can participate in this process if you want. I urge you to do so. God's pruning in your life means only one thing: he sees your fruitfulness and wants to increase it. Thanking God for the abrasive person or difficult circumstance won't come naturally at first, but it's the path to accelerated growth. Cultivate an attitude of teachability. Stay in a posture of humility.

How do you embrace people the Lord uses to prune you? Ask, "Lord, what can I learn from this person and from all my colleagues and authority figures? What are you preparing me for with their presence?"

Don't miss that last bit. All pruning is *preparation*. All character cutting is for growth.

THE PURPOSE OF PRUNING

Pruning is to prepare you for more capacity, both in the kingdom and within your spirit. The preparation isn't always in the form of an abrasive colleague. It could also look like a special work project you didn't ask for, an assignment you don't feel is your responsibility, or a job you feel unqualified for. But guess what? You don't grow when you are comfortable. Remember growing pains from your childhood? If we desire to find our purpose, we must cultivate an awareness of any preparation the Lord is doing in us. We stay on the lookout for what is odd.

As you go through every meeting, every task, every day, ask the Father, "What are you working toward?" This is the spiritual equivalent of going to work with Dad. There is nothing quite as fun.

Let him show you his approach and the mastery and wisdom in his decisions and tactfulness. He may prompt you to speak when you'd rather be silent. He may give you love for the lost when they seem to be out of reach. He may give you wisdom you've never had because you've never been in a situation where you've needed it. His guidance will come to mean something specific for you.

Start every day with an awareness that the Spirit inhabits all situations. He is in every moment, and he'd like for you to be just as present. When you practice this situational awareness, he will let you participate in the fun of kingdom building.

As you willingly engage in the work of pruning, the Spirit will work through you, and this will cause your attitudes to change.

Your anger toward authority disappears. Your frustration with colleagues or clients is converted into appreciation. You gladly suffer the loss of the things of this world (your preferences and privileges) in anticipation of what the Lord might give you to do. It's a wonderful thing. Wrenches and worship begin to go hand in hand.

Some smart people have called this "sanctification."

Ask the Lord how he tends the garden you work within—the company you serve, the job you keep, the business you own. This is where the real fun begins. This is where you discover the joy of working with the Lord.

OR ARE YOU BEING PLANTED?

While pruning is about the removal of things that prevent growth, planting is about letting good things grow.

Planting is vision. Planting is faith in the future. When you plant something, you do so because you see potential even before the living thing exists. It's the ability to look at an apple seed and see the fully grown apple tree in your mind.

You can participate in God's planting work in your life. Simply ask the Almighty what your strengths are. These could be skills, virtues, gifts, or vocational talent. Strengths are the things you know you do well. Then, with the strengths God has given you, take initiative where others don't.

Look for opportunities to apply those strengths at work. Sometimes there will be a direct connection with the great task God is doing, and you'll be able to apply those strengths to bring relief to the oppressed. At other times you'll know only that you're faithfully applying your strengths as unto the Lord, but you won't yet have a clear idea of how he wants to use them.

You can offer your strengths to your job as an act of faithful initiative, even if you find yourself in a work environment that is not ideal or in a business that is not flourishing.

Friend, do not hoard what the Lord has given you. Do not save your strengths for companies or bosses you think are more deserving. Consider Jesus' perspective: "If you love only those who love you, what reward is there for that?" (Matt. 5:46 NLT). Never hold out on giving your strengths because you're waiting for a more faith-friendly atmosphere. Doing so will cause your strengths to die on the vine.

If God is the one providing for you, then this job is what God has for you right now. He wants you applying your strengths to whatever situation you're in. Initiative is the spiritual act of watering the work the Lord has given you.

God is glorified in your growth. So plant your giftedness, sprinkled with the love of Jesus, in every opportunity you can. Purpose is something you do, not something you receive. Purpose comes when you act in faith in each task at work with the expectation of harvest. This is how you participate in the good that God is causing all things to work toward.

THE PURPOSE OF PLANTING

Let's start with purpose. Yours, to be specific. Your personal purpose, the reason you exist, is *to know and experience the Lord*. In his goodness. In his grandeur. In his love. And as his servant.

But purpose is a big pool to swim in, so let's focus on *fulfillment*. Fulfillment is a measure of how satisfied you are with your purpose. Fulfillment happens when we are happy with where we are in the realization of purpose. Really, the only time we question our purpose is when we are low on fulfillment. Which is why a man's work is so important to God.

Fulfillment grows richer and more nuanced through the years as you learn to better align with God's great task. When you look back through your life, you want to be able to say "That was the Lord" or "Lord, look what we did together!" These are the trail markers of fulfillment.

Many men feel unfulfilled, though they would never say it. They might not be able to recognize that they're feeling this way, but they can certainly know it when they find themselves waiting for five o'clock. Sometimes this is because they think that any time they spend with the Lord will happen outside working hours. Perhaps they've made no memories with him within the working day. Because this connection with God—what we might call "practical communion"—is absent from their day, so is fulfillment.

It is a lie that you must enjoy what you do in order to feel fulfilled at work. Fulfillment comes from alignment with purpose, not from external things like working conditions, job perks, salary, title, coworkers, or enjoying the actual tasks of the work. Fulfillment is a by-product of relationship with the Lord. Work is a social experience meant to be done with the One who invented it. If you have no memories of working *with* the Lord in something, then you'll always be looking for the next job and hoping that the next sale or business opportunity will bring you fulfillment.

Paul said, "I know how to live on almost nothing or with everything. I have learned the secret of living in every situation, whether it is with a full stomach or empty, with plenty or little" (Phil. 4:12 NLT). He knew the benefit of working with the Lord, and he'd learned it while in custody. He'd practiced initiative during imprisonment. But we see evidence of this attitude throughout his life.

Whether he was making tents, lecturing, being kept in prison, or preaching the gospel, his fulfillment was connected to his faith and his purpose. He knew that if he showed up, he could expect to see the Lord there as well. You can always expect to see God "punch in" before you do. I find that hugely encouraging.

Jesus said, "I came that they may have life and have it abundantly" (John 10:10). The abundance he brings is much larger than the job you hold or the amount of money you get paid. It's true that you should work together with him on the dreams he's given you. That's part of the fun. But fulfillment is by no means confined to what you do. Fulfillment at work and within your calling is directly linked to how you abide in Christ on the job.

Life is the container of your affections and desires and God's promises. So long as your desire is to keep God involved, you will see the passions he's planted and the promises he's made become a reality in your life. We turn our affections toward him not to earn his abundance but because he gives to us so abundantly.

DO YOU HAVE THE MIND OF CHRIST?

God is drawing all people to himself—you included (see John 12:32). As you learn to recognize his call, your ambitions will become clearer.

Reflect for a moment on what it means to have "the mind of Christ" (1 Cor. 2:16). One of the things it means is that Christians have been given a mind-set that agrees with God's nature. It also means that Christians have dreams and ambitions that give glory to the One who created dreams and ambitions in the first place.

You may feel a gentle tug as you read this: a reminder of an idea, dream, or ambition the Lord planted in you. Perhaps it's been growing for quite some time. It will grow faster as you embrace situational awareness and participate in the pruning and planting God is doing in your work life.

Take courage: God does not plant dead things. If you're being pruned or planted, it's evidence that he sees great potential in you. He intends what he has planted in you to grow to fruition.

Now, fruition may not mean that all your dreams come true. God never promised that. For any of us, fruition means forward motion. It means seeing the things that God planted begin to bear fruit in our lives.

The reason God gives you ambitions is that he wants you to take pleasure in watching him accomplish what he's planted in your heart. Godly ambitions will cause you to trust him. Who else could plant such a vision in you and also cause it to become a reality?

As you cooperate with the Spirit's pruning and planting, you will begin to see abundance within your work. Not the world's definition of abundance, maybe, but God's definition. The Lord's abundance looks like more of him—which means more life, the fruit of which is more freedom, more meaningful relationships, and more goodness. The fruit of the Spirit. Characteristics of our Creator.

When you work with him, you get paid twice. Every two weeks in the form of a paycheck and every day in the form of the abundance his nature creates. This is the richness of his love. The abundance of his joy. Working with him creates an overflow in your heart that will propel you through the day.

What a joy it is to know him! To work with him and to love him. He is both what drives us and what we are driven toward. All glory belongs to him.

Daily Prayer

Father, you are a good gardener. Thank you for planting vision and virtue within me.

Teach me how to take godly initiative during the day. Show me how to participate in what you're doing in me to plant good things in my life, in my career, and in the lives of my colleagues.

Show me also where you are pruning dead things in my life. Thank you for clipping back the things in my heart that don't give glory to you and that prevent me from experiencing the new things you want to move me into. I trust you.

I trust that you are working all things for my good. I trust that the people and situations you bring into my life are for my benefit. Thank you for being so willing to live with me and work with me during the working hours of the day.

Create a new perspective in me that welcomes your companionship. Even when I am busy with responsibility, help me be aware of your Spirit and what you are doing in me today.

In Christ, amen.

Chapter 8

THE PRISON AND THE PRESENCE

Who has despised the day of small things?
—Zechariah 4:10 NASB

I should've been happy with where I was, but I wanted to make a change.

I was twenty-six, a vice president, and I'd recently sold my company to my current employer. My situation was good. I had a loft downtown, a luxury car, and all the creature comforts I could want.

But I felt a little lost. I wondered, *God, is this all there is for me?* I was frustrated with my job. I was frustrated with my boss. I was even frustrated with the amount of money I made. I longed for something bigger, something more significant maybe, and I wondered whether I needed to cut loose from where I was and go looking for it.

Then, as I walked into my office one morning, the Lord told me, "I'm placing you in an incubator."

It was an interesting word—*incubator*. It came out of the blue. The message gave me comfort. Though I was unhappy in the moment, I had the sense that I shouldn't obey my urge to go looking for fulfillment somewhere else. I felt that God had me here to grow me, to incubate me, even as he used me where I was.

Later that week, my boss asked to meet with me. He opened our discussion with these curious words: "I'm placing you in a business incubator."

You can imagine my reaction. But I didn't say anything.

"I've come up with a new term," he said. "*Business incubator*. I want you to manage your department as if it operates independently from the rest of the company. You'll be in charge of its growth and processes regardless of any larger plan or direction we take."

Suddenly the Lord's words clicked. There were hugely important things happening right where I was, and I'd been about to fly the coop! As much as I wanted to transition, God wanted me to grow. If I had left, I would have taken all my issues with me. Leaving would have led me to a repeat of the discontentment I was experiencing. Encouraged that God knew what he was doing (shocker, right?), I embraced the new responsibility with as much energy as I had resisted it at first.

For the next two years, as I concentrated on serving the Lord where he'd placed me, I learned and grew immensely. It happened that I was able to take on more responsibilities as time progressed, but I had the strong feeling that this wasn't what God was interested in. What God was interested in was how well I stayed present to the work he'd called me to do. My work—then and now—is ministry to him and to others. And that ministry increased as I stayed diligent in the here and now of holy labor.

Had I not been willing to embrace the incubation that the Lord set before me, there's a good chance I wouldn't have been equipped for new work he later called me to do. And if I'd embraced that discontentment, I certainly wouldn't have had a hopeful attitude toward my situation.

IS THIS ALL THERE IS?

Have you ever been in that spot, feeling as if there must be something more for you than what you're experiencing now? I have—more than once.

When we read the Bible, we see these amazing heroes of the faith doing incredible things in the power of God. It's natural for the Christian man to think, *Wow, what I wouldn't give to be used by God like that.* Then we look at our own situations, and we remember that, no, we're not actually walking on water. Or raising the dead. Or moving mountains. We're just punching a time card. The disconnect between what we'd like to see in our lives and what we actually see can start to get to us.

Sometimes there's a nonspiritual aspect to the "more" we feel God has promised us. Whether the idea comes from our own minds or from false teaching or from somewhere else, we can come to think that God has promised us elevation in every way here on earth. We can even start to think that the calling God has for us is supposed to include better pay, more impressive titles, and more visible roles.

We can take 1 Corinthians 2:9—"What no eye has seen, nor ear heard, nor the heart of man imagined, what God has prepared for those who love him"—to mean that God intends his children to have great earthly wealth, power, and honor. We can think that if we have enough faith, God will certainly raise us more and more as our lives go on.

If we have encountered that sort of teaching and when we look at our lives and jobs and see a different reality, it can really start to chafe. As the serpent knew all the way back in the garden of Eden, a really good way to lead humans into sin is to convince them they don't have what they are *owed*.

So many Christian men are unhappy in their jobs. If they were perfectly frank, many would even admit they hate their jobs. It's so difficult when we feel that God has called us to something important and then find that our actual situations don't match up. It's difficult to feel that you're in a holding pattern or a season of waiting. It's difficult when you desire to do big things for God yet "all" you're doing is riding a jackhammer or pushing a pencil.

The discontentment can begin to eat at you. It will spill into your other relationships, including with your loved ones. It will have an impact on your effectiveness on the job, and it will sure make Monday morning—or Wednesday at 1:37—feel like prison. It will also affect your coworkers. Who hasn't been around someone who is miserable in his or her job? That person's misery drags everyone down.

But what choice does a man in this situation have? He's a priest. He's a king. He's born-again royalty. But his job is to pick up people's trash. He volunteered to be God's man to do great things for the kingdom of God, yet his day consists of enduring the tirades of angry customers.

It's no surprise that Christian men around the world look up and say, "Lord, is this really all there is for me? Didn't you have something bigger for me to do?"

HERE COMES THAT DREAMER

Joseph was more familiar than most of us with this question. He was a normal guy, but his story is exceptional. There may be no better average Joe (pun intended) story in the Bible with a more dramatic rise-fall-rise sequence. Some of Joseph's hardships were of his own making, and some he had no say in. A look at Joseph's life is a great way to talk about finding God's calling in the job you have.

Joseph had dreams from God that indicated he would rise above his brothers and parents. So, being immature but wanting to try to bring those dreams to pass, he told his family about the dreams (see Gen. 37:5–10).

Maybe we can't blame him. What's a guy to do who is told by God that he's destined to do great things? What should our actions be if our current situations don't appear to jibe with what God has called us to?

It will always be hard to do your best at work when you feel as if something's wrong with where you are now and that something better is out there somewhere else.

In fact, that might actually be a pretty good definition of discontentment.

When Joseph had these dreams and told them to his family, maybe he was just innocently reporting what he'd seen. Maybe he was naive about how it would sound to them. Or maybe he was trying to reconcile his current situation with his dream and pull the two into alignment.

THE GAP

Most of us would love to experience Moses moments, points when we could say that the Red Sea moved for our families, our friends, or our faith. We long to make history with our Maker—or to at least have a time or two when we felt we participated in the work the Lord was doing in the world.

But as we get older or as life simply gets busy, the gap between career and calling seems to become larger and larger. Some guys, no doubt, feel they could drive a boat between the two.

If we've had mountaintop experiences with God, then the time spent back at base camp can seem like a real letdown. This might even be true of our entire Christian lives, as if the moment of salvation was the mountaintop experience and everything since has been a downer.

Consider the beginning of Saul's called career: "The Spirit of the LORD will rush upon you, and you will prophesy with them and be turned into another man. Now when these signs meet you, do what your hand finds to do, for God is with you" (1 Sam. 10:6–7).

Most of us have experienced a "Lord-rushed" moment. Or a time when we were turned into another man. "Born again," as the Scriptures say (John 3:7; 1 Pet. 1:3). After that, we can begin to feel that we've been left to fend for ourselves. We know we're saved—no issues there—but the question lingers: What does a man do with his new life? Isn't there a purpose for him in this life after salvation?

He could try to be a good Christian. He could wear Christian things or watch Christian media. He could even get a fish-symbol bumper sticker so the world knows he has really changed his tune.

Somehow, though, the changes don't seem to stick. That stresses us. So we try harder. Or work harder. Or if we're desperate, we worship harder—all in an effort to stem the tide of how we feel about how we function during the day. To make matters worse, some of us have been taught that this stress is part of a man's mantle. And if something doesn't seem right about his spiritual condition, then he should just buck up.

Consider young Joseph. He had a mountaintop experience in which God obviously called him to some pretty great things. Yet after he told his dreams of glory to his brothers, they threw him into a pit. Not exactly the heights he thought were in his future. The disconnect between the two must've been jarring for him. Then his own brothers sold him—they accepted cash in exchange for the ownership of him—and started cooking up a story about him being eaten by a lion or something (see Gen. 37:18–33). He didn't even have his special robe to prove that he was loved once.

Is that where you find yourself? Are you standing in the valley between your salvation and your calling? Are you sitting in base camp, looking at the mountaintop and wishing you could get back up there?

If so, you're not alone. Many Christian men feel that there is a terrible gap between what they thought the Christian life was going to be and what it seems to actually be. For most men, this frustration is especially pronounced within the work they do.

My brother, I have good news for you: *there is no gap.* There is no valley. There is no disconnect. Nothing has gone wrong. You have not been left to find your own way. You're right where you're supposed to be. And we're going to see this clearly in the life of Joseph.

JOSEPH DIDN'T WAIT

There he was, loaded like a sack of potatoes onto one of the Midianites' camels. More likely, bound by the wrists and made to stumble along behind. This young man had never lived even one day in hardship like this. He had been raised in privilege and comfort. This was a rude awakening for him.

But it was an awakening.

Things were not going as planned. No sheaves of grain were bowing to him, as his dream showed. No sun and moon were bowing to him either. What had gone wrong? Had God made a mistake?

Had his life gone off the rails? He hadn't heard his brothers' taunting words, but his thoughts were probably similar: "[Now] we will see what will become of his dreams" (Gen. 37:20).

As you look at your job, how does it seem now? So many Christian men feel that they're just doing the dog paddle as they wait for God to call them into the bigger works. That belief—that what's going on now doesn't matter as much as what will be happening later—may actually be the thing causing the discontent that many men experience nearly every day at their jobs.

We all want a calling from God, and we all imagine ourselves taking part in the Lord's tremendous deeds on the earth. We would love to believe we could find some of that—if not a whole lot of it—in our day jobs. But we look around and find that our job description is not mover of mountains or he of great faith. Instead, it's janitor. Uber driver. Gym teacher. Analyst. Even a title like VP or CEO can feel empty if we don't see God in it.

We long for God to move us to the place where he can use us in mighty ways.

The wise man understands that God already has.

Consider your own situation or the case of someone else who has felt miserable at a job because he thinks that God has passed him by or that he's just not in a position to serve God or be part of a calling where he is. How does any of this resonate?

If God's great task is always about the Great Commission, about "on earth as it is in heaven" (Matt. 6:10), what is blocking you from being part of that great task right now? If our calling is part of Jesus' monumental work in the world and if his mission now is the same as it was when he walked the streets of Jerusalem, then you are 100 percent in your calling wherever you go.

Just like Joseph, when you believe that God has called you to big things, you can choose to see your present situation as being part of those big things that the Lord needs you to give your all to right now.

Think about your job right now. Think about the people you work with and come into contact with. Can you—*will* you—choose to see it as God's called career for you? Even if nothing changes and no "big" things ever come, will you embrace it as the precise place God needs one of his best servants to be?

I JUST REMEMBERED WHAT I FORGOT

If Joseph had been thinking that this time as a slave was not really important to God, then he might've started feeling badly used or forgotten. He might've gotten bitter or begun to think he deserved some fun to compensate for all the injustices done to him. And there was the perfect opportunity all but chasing him around the house. His master's wife made a pass at him, but when Joseph refused her, she accused him to her husband, who happened to be in charge of the prison (see Gen. 39:6–19).

> Joseph's master took him and put him into the
> prison, the place where the king's prisoners were

confined, and he was there in prison. But the LORD
was with Joseph and showed him steadfast love
and gave him favor in the sight of the keeper of the
prison. And the keeper of the prison put Joseph in
charge of all the prisoners who were in the prison.
Whatever was done there, he was the one who did
it. The keeper of the prison paid no attention to
anything that was in Joseph's charge, because the
LORD was with him. And whatever he did, the LORD
made it succeed. (vv. 20–23)

Here we see Joseph behaving justly yet getting mistreated. He
seems to have learned his lesson and wasn't rubbing anyone's nose in
anything, as he'd done with his brothers. Yet he was still thrown into
a pit but of another kind.

Once again, Joseph had an opportunity to complain about his
situation and wonder where God was in it all. Yet, once again, Joseph
chose to serve God with all his heart right where he was, considering
the tasks he now had to perform, the people he now encountered,
and the authority he was now under to all have been selected for him
by God. This *was* his calling.

As before, Joseph's good choices about his job situation, as it
were, led to great blessing. We get the sense that even if he had never
left this prison, he would have been content to serve God there the
rest of his days, always giving his all and believing that God had
placed him there on purpose.

Because he was so mindful of the people he encountered even in that dark place and because he saw each person as worthy of love and respect, he served even the prisoners around him.

He encountered two prisoners who had, until recently, been servants of Pharaoh himself. One had been the chief baker, and the other had been the chief cupbearer (or butler). Both had offended Pharaoh in some way, so here they were in prison, awaiting their fate (see Gen. 40).

While checking on them one morning, Joseph learned that they'd both had strange dreams. Because Joseph, "that dreamer" (37:19 NIV), considered himself something of an expert on the subject, he asked them to tell their dreams. God gave him interpretations of the dreams: the cupbearer would soon be returned to his position, and the baker (sorry, man) was going to be executed.

These things both came to pass. The cupbearer was so excited to return to his post that he forgot all about Joseph, this amazing man who had a special power from God. For two years he forgot him.

Until one day when someone else had a mysterious dream. And then the cupbearer conked himself on the forehead and said some vital words.

> Then the chief cupbearer said to Pharaoh, "I remember my offenses today. When Pharaoh was angry with his servants and put me and the chief baker in custody in the house of the captain of the guard, we dreamed on the same night, he and I, each having a dream with its own interpretation.

A young Hebrew was there with us, a servant of the captain of the guard. When we told him, he interpreted our dreams to us, giving an interpretation to each man according to his dream. And as he interpreted to us, so it came about. I was restored to my office, and the baker was hanged."

Then Pharaoh sent and called Joseph, and they quickly brought him out of the pit. And when he had shaved himself and changed his clothes, he came in before Pharaoh. And Pharaoh said to Joseph, "I have had a dream, and there is no one who can interpret it. I have heard it said of you that when you hear a dream you can interpret it." Joseph answered Pharaoh, "It is not in me; God will give Pharaoh a favorable answer." (41:9–16)

The CEB version renders the cupbearer's words like this: "Today I've just remembered my mistake" (v. 9). After two years of blissful forgetfulness, something jogged the cupbearer's memory, and he mentioned Joseph to the king at a pivotal moment in history.

God gave Joseph an interpretation of the dream, and this led to an avalanche of change for him. Pharaoh took Joseph's advice about how to save all Egypt, released Joseph from prison and made him second in command of the kingdom, and later authorized Joseph to bring his entire family to live in the choicest spot of Egypt. Along the way, Joseph's brothers did indeed bow to him and his father heeded his call to join him (see 41:25–46:34).

MORE THAN BLOOMING

It would be tempting to say that Joseph's calling finally, at this late hour, came to pass. We might look at the story and say that everything else was just preparation for that big thing God was going to do.

But that would be to miss the point. Joseph was in his calling *the entire time*. With every fall and rise, Joseph was doing the big thing God had called him to. Serving the Lord wherever he was, under the authority of whomever he was under, and with whatever people he was with *was* the calling. Yes, he eventually did that in a more visible way, but this was merely an extension of what he'd already been doing.

Joseph didn't need to know he was going to save Egypt before he would agree to start serving God in the pit or the prison. He didn't believe that a divine calling could be fulfilled only on the main stage. He knew that any job he had at any moment was his because God had strategically placed him in it. Not merely as a waiting season in which he might learn things for later use, but to be God's special agent who was present and mindful right where he was.

Talk about blooming where you're planted. Joseph had every right to simply clock in. The situation certainly required nothing of him. No one had asked him to lead in his master's house or in that prison. No one had forced him to use his administrative skills. No one had asked him to bring his A game. But he did.

Whenever there was something to do, "he was the one who did it" (39:22). Everywhere he went, he stayed present to the situation.

He added value. He stayed present to the fact that there is no job the Lord is not in control of or involved in.

You're not in a season when you're unable to serve God. You're not. Now, you could tell yourself that you deserve better. You could say that your manager keeps you in a jail-like situation. You could throw a pity party for yourself until things change. But all that would do is make you (and those around you) miserable.

Joseph's ticket out of jail was a direct result of his understanding that his mission was always right where he was. He would have completely missed the opportunity if his heart hadn't already been in a position to stay present to his circumstances.

You are in your calling right now, if you will awake to it. This will revolutionize your attitude about your job. "It is God who works in you, both to will and to work for his good pleasure. Do all things without grumbling or disputing" (Phil. 2:13–14).

"To will and to work for his good pleasure." What a reason to wake up. No matter where you are or what your job is, you are placed there like a chess piece by the Grand Master himself.

SEEING WITH NEW EYES

Many Christian men are unhappy with their jobs. Some job situations are legitimately awful. Some feel as if they've been thrown into a pit, sold as a slave, and then falsely accused and thrown into prison!

It's easy, in a situation like that, to start wondering whether God is ever going to have anything important for you to do. And if so, we have to wonder when that happy time is going to finally get started.

But as you've seen in the life of Joseph, no matter how awful the job or environment, the man of God is always positioned exactly where he's supposed to be. Now, if your job is illegal or immoral, then you should consider how you can get out. But if it's just not your ideal, then look at it with fresh eyes.

See it not as an accident or a waiting room but as God's job for you at this time. It may be what you do for the rest of your working life, and if so, Jesus has more there for you to do every day. See the people not as the unimportant ones you have to hang around until you finally make the big time and can really be used by God. See them as the people who most need what you can provide … and the comfort and light from the Lord you represent.

I once thought I had an existential itch to go out and find God in some other job. I once thought that, by staying, I had settled for something less than what the Lord had for me. I once thought I was in a season of waiting and preparation, meaning that the important season had yet to come. It all made me miserable and discontented.

But when I learned from Joseph that the calling I wanted was right where I was and had already begun, everything changed.

The car is never in neutral for the man who wakes up ready to stick to his called work. No matter where you want to be, rest assured that the Almighty is overseeing your life. So foster stick-to-itiveness of the Spirit. God will shift gears when you are engaged and he is ready.

Daily Prayer

Thank you, Father, for giving my life purpose. I know you are with me wherever I go.

Father, every dream you've given to me, I give back to you. I will not build a road with supplies you have not given me. Teach me to walk in the awareness of you. Teach me to live out your calling every day in every job. I'll walk in obedience.

I worship you, God. You are a master builder. I marvel at your work. Thank you for incubating me even as you use me.

Help me today to see the ways in which we are working together on your great task.

I'll dream alongside you, Father.

In Christ, amen.

Chapter 9

THE POSTURE AND THE PAVEMENT

What do you have that you did not receive? If then you
received it, why do you boast as if you did not receive it?

—1 Corinthians 4:7

"Holy Spirit, fill me."

I was alone in my bed, staring at the ceiling around 11:00 p.m. I'd spent the day at a church event and had come away with a single burning conviction: *God is not as important in my work life as I want him to be.*

I knew I needed a different result, so I prayed a different prayer.

Instantly something like an invisible hand the size of my body covered me. The experience felt almost like an electric shock, though it wasn't painful. I did, however, bounce off the bed.

What happened next is still hard to explain.

For hours I sobbed, worshipping Jesus and repenting of sin. I was completely overcome. And the more overcome I became, the stronger the sense of the Lord's presence in and around me grew.

For the first time in my life, I was completely present to the reality that God was in the room. And each time I thought the experience was over, it would start again, like a wind gust on a March afternoon.

Maybe this all sounds kind of nice. But make no mistake: I was terrified.

God had shown up so quickly, so undeniably, that I had to face the reality that he was more present than I gave him credit for. This quite literally put the fear of God in me. The idea that he can, at any time, physically intervene with a man as broken as me still marks my thinking.

This experience created in me a deeply reverent posture in the work I do.

His hand is on everything, even when we don't see, feel, or understand it. Our response to his present power should be to cultivate supernatural humility in our daily work. We must develop a reverent, prostrate posture toward his righteousness. In other words, we bow our work lives.

Lower. Lower. Lower still. Your heart's posture should be so low. You should be so slow to speak and so quick to listen to the Spirit's direction. He has been so kind. He has been so generous to you with the gift of work. It is a manifold blessing. It provides for you, refines you, and relates you to the Father. Only a good God could create such a good thing.

Whatever form work takes for us is irrelevant—we never make light of manna, regardless of the way it comes. Whether it finds us in life's desert or the promised land, it is divinely made and given by heaven's hand. If we have to scoop up heaven's bread in a hard hat, so be it. It is evidence of his kindness.

Simply put, we most often see God's provision through our jobs. Work is the reality of his love. A staff that parts the Red Sea will typically look like a humble stick anyway. We don't judge the amount of the Lord's favor by the impressiveness (or lack thereof) of a project we've been given. We don't think God loves us more if he gives us an amazing work upgrade, and we don't grumble about a gift just because we don't like the wrapping paper.

In our vocations, God partners with us to advance his kingdom. It is through the work of our hands, being led by *his* hand, that we participate in this mystery.

By the way, it's healthy to recognize this as a mystery. By definition, as his kingdom advances through our work, so do we. But kingdom advancement doesn't look the same for every man. God has his own ends in mind. People look at the outward appearances of advancement, but God is focused on advancement of the heart (see 1 Sam. 16:7).

We can be sure of one thing: as we embrace the heart of the Father, our hearts for the Father's work will increase. That moves every man in a different direction. Some men move through their work lives in a linear fashion: intern, junior, senior, manager, executive, done. Their work lives are like chess games; they're always looking for the next best move. It's a strategy that works well for them.

Other men have a path that looks more like checkers. They move diagonally for a few moves; then they switch directions, hop a couple of steps, and switch directions again. God is fully involved in this mode of operating as well.

God's head is always in the game—and he will always advance us into greater kingdom work according to the way he uniquely made each of us. You can be sure that, whichever way you go about your work life, God will promote you into the place of service where he wants you as you work alongside him. The promoting may not look like how the world thinks those things should look, but God has his goals in mind.

In general, the Lord gives us agency to choose how we want to play the game. I call it a game because Christ-centered work is meant to be challenging—and fun. Not only that, but the Christian man should also see earthly work and kingdom work as being linked. No matter the way we move, God's growth plan is the best offer on the table. Because it's an offer, we treat it with humility.

The best part about God's growth plan for your called career is that it gets continuously better. But it's important to know that "better" does not always equate directly to titles and promotions. It equates to greater opportunity to do the kingdom work you were designed to do. If titles are helpful, God may lend them to you.

Said another way, the biblical idea of moving "from glory to glory" has legs (2 Cor. 3:18 NASB). It's headed somewhere. I've gone from vice president to jobless and from jobless to overseer. I've gone from full-time ministry to part-time construction worker too. But I was always advancing in my called career.

My awareness of God and partnership with him has, in general, advanced over time. Sometimes that's meant I've needed ongoing faith that he would provide a salary. Other times my faith was put to other uses while God provided a more typical means of income. But both I and the kingdom were always advancing.

This requires a certain type of humility. It requires the recognition that God provides for and promotes each of us in a different way. We need to accept how he deals with us and how he deals (differently) with the colaborers of Christ around us. Some people he will promote in the world's eyes, and other people he will not. All are equally loved by God.

There's a debate I've seen too many times within the church. One side says that earthly success shows God's love and favor. The other side says that we see God's favor most when we are lowly in terms of earthly success. The moment we say that promotion in the kingdom looks like poverty, we've taken a step back in our understanding of how God advances his children. But the second we say that promotion in the kingdom looks like a bigger paycheck, well, we're again twisting the way God works.

Both arguments are losers, and people waste way too much time on them. I've lived both perspectives, at the extremes, and I can say that neither one changes the nature of kingdom work. Money is moot in light of God's plan for our lives.

God is sovereign. Though if you ask me, even saying he's sovereign isn't putting him high enough. A word like *sovereign* tries to put a cap on just how much say he has in everything. We can't fathom his true glory. God's sovereignty gives him say-so in how promotion, both in the natural and in the spiritual, ultimately works for every one of us.

It's good for our souls to cultivate this perspective. The Bible has a name for this cultivation: it's called the fear of the Lord. We need to know that no advancement of any kind happens without it.

PAVEMENT PAVER

The fear of the Lord appears in your life in the form of humility. Humility paves the road ahead of you no matter where your career and calling take you. Humility prevents spiritual stop signs. Humility will work your inner man's muscles, preparing him to shoulder the load the Almighty might give. Every other path will distance you from the Master Builder. "Have this mind among yourselves, which is yours in Christ Jesus, who, though he was in the form of God, did not count equality with God a thing to be grasped" (Phil. 2:5–6).

Christ Jesus, the Son of God and CEO of heaven, did not count equality with God as something to be clung to. Of course, he was equal with God. He is God and he was with God in the beginning (see John 1:1–2). Yet he did not tighten his grip on his title or status. His posture toward his position was surrender. His identity, in part, was sonship.

All work is a gift. It is given by someone else and received by you. No raise was won, no interview was aced, and no position was ever secured without the Almighty's hand in it. "We are his workmanship" (Eph. 2:10)—and any promotion is part of that. As a wise king once said, "The lot is cast into the lap, but its every decision is from the LORD" (Prov. 16:33).

The Enemy loves to breed dissatisfaction in the hearts of God's people. This has been his favorite tool from the beginning. For this reason the Enemy will try to lure you into discontentment about what you do.

I find this ironic. Work is a natural part of life. We do not become discontent with the air we breathe or the hearts that pump blood to our lungs. Labor is no less essential. It is no less a blessing in our lives. We wouldn't curse our lungs, so why would we complain about a nine-to-five job, business struggles, or working the late shift?

We must elevate work to the level of a sacrament. Work is sacred, and until we see it as such, we will never be able to have the view of work that God has and we will never be able to understand the holy treasure he has given us in our jobs.

Consider this proverb: "Humility is the fear of the LORD; its wages are riches and honor and life" (Prov. 22:4 NIV). Humility *is* the fear of the Lord. The cart follows the horse. You have nothing that you have not first been given to steward. You have no talent that wasn't tallied before you were born. You have no leadership that wasn't lent to you for a limited time. So in this sense it pays to develop humility.

There were billions of men before you, and there may be billions after. How can any man lay claim to an accomplishment in his life as if it were earned on his own? It is all kindness from your King. To claim otherwise is not only untrue; it is also a deviation from the fear of the Lord.

King Solomon said, "It is good for people to eat, drink, and enjoy their work under the sun during the short life God has given them" (Eccl. 5:18 NLT). God desires you to enjoy work. That should be great news to us all. Or a wake-up call. If you have found a measure of contentment, then that is as real a blessing as a man can receive in life.

Being humble is a funny thing. It's reward enough on its own. But according to Proverbs, humility is the fear of the Lord, and the fear of the Lord pays wages of riches, honor, and life (see 22:4 NIV). If our goal is ever to have riches and honor on this earth, that may make them fly away on the wings of an eagle (see Prov. 23:4–5). But true fear of the Lord will bring some of those extra blessings too.

But having riches, honor, and life can be a snare. When not stewarded well, these things can erode your contentment. So, for your part, never graduate from a facedown posture before the Lord. Say instead with the angels, "Holy, holy, holy is the LORD Almighty" (Isa. 6:3 NIV). The song of your heart should be a humble hymn on repeat: "I will not presume on the Lord." His graces, however abundant they may be, are just that: *his* graces.

If you have work to do and you are humbly grateful to God for it, it is a testimony to your posture. Honest work is evidence of his delight. No matter what work you find yourself doing in life, you are always a son of his house. Being a son brings an inheritance, and part of that grace is labor. By grace you are grafted into heaven's family. A new branch with a holy Brother. May you never stray far from the Father's hand.

Remember, you are already seated in heavenly places (see Eph. 2:6). If your job or your place in life feels a little too low, remember your reality. You have been promoted to a spiritual location and *vocation*. No matter what your earthly position, your spiritual position is greater. You are a knight kneeling before his King, ever thankful for the saving grace that works its way through your earthly work.

How do you build up the fear of the Lord within yourself? How do you stay facedown in every work reality in which you find yourself?

Begin with *gratitude*. Write a list of love on your heart—a set of things you're grateful for. Remember that everything you have has, in fact, been given to you. *Everything* means "everything." Your personality, your temperament, your education, your talent, and your opportunities. And if these have been given to us, we can't strut around as though we gave them to ourselves.

There is a sovereign hand over your life, the same hand I felt over me that night after the prayer event. It is so holy and high above you. It was intentional as it crafted every atom within you. From head to toe and from heart to task, you were created with wonderful capableness.

In nearly every way you could conceive, you are made in the image of your Maker. Welded in the womb (see Ps. 139:13). Your skills are even a sort of reflection of his heavenly talent. They exist because of the Almighty's desire to use you in his great task and because of his will to give you good things. Everything good—or capable of *the* good—comes from the Lord's own goodness.

Once you have made a mental list of the attributes of the Almighty you find in yourself, you can get busy building humility into everything you do. Humility is a discipline that strengthens your capability. Advancement of any kind is predicated on the way you posture yourself within your present work environment.

AMAZING THINGS

Real humility starts with remembrance. Consider the story of Joshua and the Jordan River.

Many years ago, on the bank of that ancient river, a nation and its leader needed to cross over into the future God had promised them. At this point, Joshua, the nation's commander, was probably one of the few people who could remember this nation, with different people, miraculously crossing a great body of water once before. Miracles were in his memory. And this memory enabled him to act confidently as he went about his work.

> "As soon as you see the ark of the covenant of the LORD your God being carried by the Levitical priests, then you shall set out from your place and follow it. Yet there shall be a distance between you and it, about 2,000 cubits in length. Do not come near it, in order that you may know the way you shall go, for you have not passed this way before." Then Joshua said to the people, "Consecrate yourselves, for

tomorrow the LORD will do wonders among you."
(Josh. 3:3–5)

The NIV says, "The LORD will do amazing things among you" (v. 5).

Though the children of Israel had never gone that way before, the nation crossed over the river without a hitch. As Joshua had said, it truly was an amazing thing—in part, because this man of God had done his job well. His posture toward the Almighty and his remembrance of what the Lord had done for them forty years prior made this new miracle just another day on the job.

Joshua walked in the fear of the Lord.

Then he went a step further. Until this point, he was calling to mind only his own remembrance of what the Lord had done in the past. But this ability to remember God's deeds needed to be given to the whole nation. So, with the Lord's guidance, Joshua had the people construct a riverside memorial to remind them of the things God had done that day. He did this so that both he and the nation of Israel would remember the way the Lord had provided for them. They would need this memory to fall back on the next time they were tempted to question the Lord's faithfulness.

> Those twelve stones, which they took out of the Jordan, Joshua set up at Gilgal. And he said to the people of Israel, "When your children ask their fathers in times to come, 'What do these stones mean?' then you shall let your children know, 'Israel passed over this Jordan on dry ground.' For

> the LORD your God dried up the waters of the
> Jordan for you until you passed over, as the LORD
> your God did to the Red Sea, which he dried up
> for us until we passed over, so that all the peoples
> of the earth may know that the hand of the LORD
> is mighty, that you may fear the LORD your God
> forever." (4:20–24)

Great rivers can't be crossed without a great God. Neither can you cross confidently into whatever your calling requires of you without his hand. It all starts with the fear of the Lord: "The hand of the LORD is mighty, that you may fear the LORD your God forever" (v. 24). The might of his hand is what enables you to move forward in humility and faith.

MAKE MEMORIALS

Memorials are the practical part of humility.

The Israelites stacked stones from the river to remember how God had miraculously gotten them across the Jordan. A God-fearing man will stack stones of remembrance in his heart as a way of keeping the past in perspective and the future in focus. The benefit to his soul is incalculable. He will be unlikely to fall into the trap of discontentment or pride when he has a pile of memories that remind him that the Lord went before him right through life's rivers, including those faced at work.

Back to that converted oil tank I lived in years ago. My uncle had brought the oil tank from West Texas and had cut a doorway in the side, intending to use the tank for storage. I took it for myself, thrilled to have my own room away from my brothers. I scrubbed out all the oil and placed an old couch inside. Sure, there was no running water or electricity, but it kept the rain out a little better than my previous situation. Best of all, the tank gave me a place of quiet in which to practice the skills and develop the talents the Lord would later use in my life.

Though it was a small step, this is stone number one in my own pile of memorials. Whenever God moves me forward in some way, I think back to that oily beginning and I thank him for parting rivers and seas that will always be too big for me. God made provision for me in the wilderness.

Now, whenever God gives me new provision, whether work related or otherwise, I remember his kindness toward me. I stack each memory, starting with that oil tank, and thank him for the mile markers along the way. This helps me remember his steadfastness. He never once left me without a roof over my head. And he has done much more than that since. Even though I am a long way from that first rusted roof, I keep the stones from that distant riverbank. If ever I begin to think differently about God or my own role in all that's happened, this keeps me living in reality.

I maintain three tiers of remembrance: weekly, yearly, and seasonal.

Weekly remembrance focuses on cultivating a fear of the Lord. At the end of every week, on Saturday or Sunday, look back at all the things that went well or worked out.

A funny phenomenon happens to us throughout life. You'll know it because it's normally followed by the statement "Everything worked out okay" or something similar. Take time to reflect on everything that worked out during the week. Each incident is evidence that the Lord is still working out all things for the good of those who love him (see Rom. 8:28). This is the reality of the Holy Spirit orchestrating all the details of your life, including your workweek.

Start to notice the relief you feel when a situation turns out okay. That feeling is the fruit of the Spirit's presence in your life. For unbelievers, this is part of the kindness of God that may lead them to repentance (see Rom. 2:4). The reality of God taking over the details. It can be anything. Perhaps you were double-booked for a meeting and one meeting was canceled. Or maybe you were late on a project and the date was extended. All these happy little changes are God working for your good despite the craziness of the day.

Make a note of them as they occur. Thank him for all of them at the end of the week. Thanking him will remind your soul of the reality that God is involved in everything. This also has the benefit of increasing your faith since now your awareness of him will grow. He is not absent from your workweek.

Yearly remembrance is about stacking those stones. Its purpose is to build a memorial in your life of the work that the Lord has done within you and for you in the previous 365 days.

During the year, if God came through for you in some way, allowed you to minister in some way, or gave you the opportunity to lead something at work, no matter how small, write it down in a ledger or journal. Once a year, open that ledger and reflect on the faithfulness and provision God granted you throughout the year. Become aware of the ways in which you advanced or were given new opportunities.

When you take time to notice these markers, your soul will become aware of all the ways the Lord was for you. It doesn't matter whether you work for fifteen or a hundred dollars an hour. It also doesn't matter what type of work you do or the title you possess. The evidence we're looking for is that of relationship, the reality of God at work. Every year, look back at the pile of provision he's created for you.

These are the signs of faithfulness that point to the path across the riverbed. His provision can look like a change in career, a new job, or advancement in your company. It can look like favor, as with Joseph in Pharaoh's house.

God's faithfulness shows up when things take a turn for the worse too. He's just as involved when we're fired, demoted, or disfavored. His focus is always on his great task of bringing relief to the oppressed, and sometimes you're the one who needs relief.

Be aware that the Enemy would love to plant doubt, insecurity, or pride in your heart. Anything that turns your gaze from the faithfulness of the Father will create room for pride to grow. So remind yourself: nothing good and new happens only because of work you did.

To make sure you don't distance yourself from the One who granted advancement in the first place, meditate on and thank the Lord for the unique ways he has provided for you and has helped you in times past. Consider taking a day off or going on a prayerful hike for a few hours. Whatever you do, take time regularly to renew your spirit with the remembrance of the Lord's faithfulness. This habit will give you faith, encourage you when setbacks come, and keep you humble as you move into your new season of calling and career.

THE PRIDE OF LIFE

Remembrance protects your heart from the pride that comes from believing the lie that you've done something important all on your own. There is no "on my own" in a calling. God's promotion, whatever that may look like, is linked to his favor and purposes. Sadly, David had to learn this the hard way.

As you may know, David lived out a called career. He had a lifetime of memories to remind him that the Lord was the one who was at work in his life. That should've been obvious, since he started as a shepherd, became a guerrilla warrior, and was finally made king over the nation of Israel. The Lord had favor on him at each step along the way—in every role too. For the most part, he stewarded these transitions well. You have only to look at the Psalms to see that David had a discipline of dedicating himself to the Lord in praise.

There was one time, however, when he forgot he was along for the ride and not the one driving.

By the middle of David's kingship, he had already led an impressive life. He'd first defeated a lion. Then a giant. Then tribes. Finally nations. He'd also duplicated himself through leadership. He had mighty men and large armies, many of whom conquered their own lions, giants, and tribes. He had started as only a shepherd boy, way out in the boondocks of Judah's hills. He was the youngest of his brothers, last in the line of inheritance. This was all the Lord's favor. God's choice.

He seemed to forget this, though, becoming a bit full of himself and deciding to measure just how great he'd become:

> Satan stood against Israel and incited David to number Israel. So David said to Joab and the commanders of the army, "Go, number Israel, from Beersheba to Dan, and bring me a report, that I may know their number." But Joab said, "May the LORD add to his people a hundred times as many as they are! Are they not, my lord the king, all of them my lord's servants? Why then should my lord require this? Why should it be a cause of guilt for Israel?" (1 Chron. 21:1–3)

The Lord had used one man, David, to defeat the Philistines many years before. David had confessed freely that his victory over Goliath was entirely the Lord's (see 1 Sam. 17:45–47). From an early age, he had participated in God's plan, which was a huge honor. The fact that he'd later been promoted to head of state was also due to God's sovereign choice. However, after so many successes, David decided to rise from his original posture of humility.

He counted as his own those things that were his only to steward.

Joab, David's friend and one of his commanders, saw this and tried to keep him accountable: "May the LORD add to *his* people a hundred times as many" (1 Chron. 21:3). In other words, "Why count money in another man's bank account? Why look at the Lord's handiwork as if it's your own?"

The Lord may promote you past your expectation. You may gain favor, finances, and friends as outcomes of your job. You may have an army's worth of anointing for what you are called to do. Every ounce of it is the Lord's.

When we harbor pride about our accomplishments, we are essentially saying that we don't need the Almighty's governance in our lives. It's insulting to God.

For David, this resulted in a severe winnowing of his army. Ultimately he lost seventy thousand men. For you, it may mean you experience stagnation or a limit on what you can do. Pride's fall has a real-world impact.

Consider David's humility, seen here in a psalm possibly written after his decision to count the people:

> No king is saved by the size of his army;
>   no warrior escapes by his great strength.
> A horse is a vain hope for deliverance;
>   despite all its great strength it cannot save.
> But the eyes of the LORD are on those who fear him,
>   on those whose hope is in his unfailing love.
>   (Ps. 33:16–18 NIV)

Even if you aren't aware of the Lord's involvement in your achievements, that makes this reality no less real. If you obtain a breakthrough in your job or business, big or small, *the Lord did it* with your help. Remind yourself of this often.

Daily, if need be.

REPENTING OF PRIDE

David's process of repentance was profound too. It all started with an angel, an altar, and a godly guy named Ornan. At the peak of David's pain, an angel of the Lord ordered David to build an altar on another man's property (see 1 Chron. 21:18). Which, in and of itself, was humbling.

As a warrior, David could have taken the property by force. He was talented enough. He could have exercised eminent domain over the land. He was powerful enough. He also could have played the God card and told the landowner that he alone knew the spiritual key that would stop Israel's suffering. David did none of these things. He insisted on paying the full price.

However, Ornan, the owner of the land, offered David the property for free. Ornan even threw in oxen and other material for the offering as a bonus. He made it easy. A fast-food sacrifice for David. "Look, I will give the oxen for the burnt offerings, the threshing sledges for the wood, and the wheat for the grain offering. I will give all this" (v. 23 NIV).

This was a man who had zero ties to David's sin. But his posture was so reverent that even the man's sledges were up for sacrifice. He was happy to give up his means of income if it enabled the king to

do what he needed to do. David's response to this man's attitude is
no less profound: "No, I insist on paying the full price. I will not take
for the LORD what is yours, or sacrifice a burnt offering that costs me
nothing" (v. 24 NIV).

Let's focus on the last part of that verse: "or sacrifice a burnt
offering that costs me nothing." Why did David say this? Certainly
this offer would have provided a faster means to an end. To understand his thinking, it helps to ask ourselves a similar question: Why
is it so important to give the Lord an offering at our own expense?

In this moment of clarity, David knew that even though the
nation was his, he was just a steward with a few years left on the
earth. It would be inappropriate to undertake the work of repentance
with an air of entitlement. Everything David had access to was on
loan. The sacrifice was simply a confession, an acknowledgment of
this fact. "The earth is the LORD's, and everything in it," he is known
to have said in Scripture (Ps. 24:1 NIV).

The same goes for your credentials, your talent, and even your
dreams or aspirations. We might think that, by simply acting in
integrity or doing a good job, we are truly acting as a living sacrifice,
as Romans 12:1 reminds us. But we'll have missed the mark. There
is no sacrifice in giving back to the Lord what you are already good
at. He *made* you good at it. He placed the dreams in your subcon-
scious mind too. Your exaltation, from this perspective, would take
no effort.

So how do you live out your work life through empowered
penance, choosing to abstain from the patterns of this world (see
Rom. 12:1–2)?

When I was sobbing and repenting in that hotel room years ago, I wanted more than anything for the Lord to be front and center in my life at work. I made that change, and God has blessed me in innumerable ways because of it. Not least being that I knew I was where he wanted me to be and where he could use me best.

The only thing we can really give God is our hearts. And at times that gift will cost us our pride. But that's such a small price. Everything we have, every opportunity God has given us, is a generous and kind advance. He has been so gracious with us. He has loved us so well. Our work is evidence of that fact. So in return, offer your work to him with humility. Make humility a throne and let the fear of the Lord reign on it.

Daily Prayer

Father, thank you. Thank you for acting on my behalf throughout every season of my life. I acknowledge that you are the way maker and my true provider. There is no talent I have, job I've done, or opportunity in my lap that hasn't been given to me by you. I am well aware of your goodness, and I will not pretend that what I do is somehow done on my own.

You endowed me with my personality, approach, and passions. And each one, in some way, is a reflection of you. I want you to be made known through me. So I will not stifle my work with fruitless pride.

Teach me to walk humbly before you each day. Allow me also to see the finer details of how you work on my behalf.

I want to grow with you in intimacy and intention today.

In Christ, amen.

Chapter 10

THE WORK AND
THE GOOD

In all toil there is profit, but mere talk tends only to poverty.

—Proverbs 14:23

To be frank, we were up against a wall. The problem was intractable.

My client, the CEO of a large faith-based media company, was insistent on solving a communication problem within a new platform we were building. The solution, which would allow two-way conversations between people across state and regional lines, had to be implemented in a specific way.

There was both a technical challenge and an implementation constraint. I had already worked hard on the issue. Nearly forty hours had been spent trying to come up with a solution that was both elegant and practical. But so far we had found no such solution.

So I was stuck.

From an integrity perspective, I'd done fine. I had done my best and had worked hard on a way to fix the problem. But none of this effort had produced a good outcome for my client.

As we discussed alternatives, the conversation began to get heated. It became clear that none of my alternatives would be considered, yet a way had to be found.

This wasn't a time for leadership or soft skills. I needed a good idea. So as my client continued to talk, I prayerfully considered the options.

Nearly instantly the Lord showed me a way around the constraints and how to implement the solution. I cut my client off: "I've got the answer! The Lord showed me the solution."

Can I say that? I thought.

My client sounded skeptical but was happy that it seemed as if I'd found a solution. We wrapped up our meeting and I got to work.

God had shown me a hidden approach to solving the problem elegantly. It wasn't rocket science, but it also wasn't common knowledge. The solution was something that neither of us had tried or even thought of before. It was specific, technical, and confined to our problem. It also worked beautifully—exactly as God had shown it to me in the meeting. In fact, it became one of the better features of the new product.

I considered the work good not necessarily because it solved a problem but because something good was created where nothing good had existed. In a moment my client and I went from chaos to clarity. We went from hard work to good work.

Only good can come of involving God in your work. He always has a better, more creative solution in mind than what you could've come up with on your own.

GIVING YOUR BEST?

"Do your best!" echoes in the mind of every boy aged five to fifty-two. Some of us were inundated—some might even say *knighted*—with this impulse from a day much earlier than we can remember. But do we understand what the command really means?

What does it mean to do our best? We know it means not to let our fathers, our wives, or our bosses down. We know it means to leave everything on the field, be it the ball field or the boardroom. We know it means we are able to look ourselves in the eye in the mirror at night.

But what is our best? And who gets to say? If you think you've put your best foot forward, how do you know whether it's really true? Could you have done even better? Do you know the difference between a halfhearted pace of work and a hearty one?

Who can discern the difference between our best work and a job done just generally well? No one can except you. Whether you're a president or a paper pusher, the best effort you can give is effort given with integrity. After that, the Almighty is the one who measures. After all, who of us can judge his labor in the light of his own dim glory? We don't cast shadows beyond ourselves.

Which causes us to ask, Whom do we actually work for?

The Bible makes it clear: "Whatever you do, work heartily, as for the Lord and not for men" (Col. 3:23). Not a man. Not a manager. Not even ourselves. We work for the Lord.

This makes sense. God is the only one qualified to assess our work. Every other measurement of "best"—or even of "boss"—is moot.

If you work for yourself, you may be thinking, *Hey, shouldn't I get some say in what a solid day's work should be?*

No, it's not up to you.

But I work hard! you might be thinking. What is hard work, though? Is it measured by the manual labor required, brainpower expended, or time spent? Perhaps it's based on the amount of sweat and stress you experienced during the day. Or sacrifice made. Or duty performed.

At the end of the day, there is only one kind of work worth considering: good work.

Perhaps it goes without saying, but God cares about our work. He cares what we do and how we do it. He wants it to have the residue of his Spirit on it as well. Similar to the stones in the river we discussed, good work is a marker that says, "God was here." He knows that work that fits his definition of *good* is good for the soul, good for people, and good for the greater good.

Both you and those whom you serve are better for the good work you do. Good work is restorative. It causes us, even in the smallest of ways, to worship, wonder, and work out our salvation (see Phil. 2:12).

To think of it another way, if a calling is about what we're meant to do with our lives, then good work is how we go about fulfilling that calling. Good work is the tactical part of fulfilling the grand strategy we've been called to live out. In a way, it is how we abide under the banner of God's love during the working day.

But instead of doing good work, most of us have been simply told to do our best. So we try our hardest to do so. We work hard, often because it's the highest ethic we know how to live up to when we don't have a larger, existential reason for why we work. But a calling will require much more than your effort. It will require your intentionality—something that can be achieved only through the spiritual revelation of good work.

We see this clearly in the Genesis story. Better yet, we get a definition of good work.

But consider first the kind of work at the other end of the spectrum: restless work—the outcome of mindlessly "doing our best."

Hard, restless work is the world's way of doing things. This kind of work, while well meaning, is easily contaminated by the pride of life, putting an end to any godly ambition the worker might have. This defiled sense of duty will get in the way of the pure purpose we are supposed to embody as Christian men. The world has no problem trading rest for revenue (or anything else, for that matter).

However, as followers of Christ, we look at things differently. Our ambition is for salvation, good works, and life abundant (the fruit of living lives of calling). Thankfully, we have to look no further to understand good work than the origin of work—the creation story in Genesis: "God saw everything that he had made, and behold, *it was very good*" (1:31).

Now, that's impressive. Everything God made and everything he did was good. From fleas to flamingos—fauna, flora, and everything else—it was all good. Moreover, he *finished* all the work he set out to do. There were no half-finished foxes or generally good geese. No barren fields or accidentally dim stars. Everything was good. It was one impressive workweek.

One we can learn from.

WHAT IS GOOD WORK?

God gave us the perfect example of how to do good work, but so many things in our lives try to crowd out its purity. Our own sin and fallen nature cause us to look at a finished job or task and wonder, *Is it perfect? Is it world class? Is it better than my colleagues' work?* The answer to all these questions could be "Yes," yet it's still possible that none of what you did was good by biblical standards.

Consider for a moment what the state of the earth was before the Lord did his work: "The earth was without form and void, and darkness was over the face of the deep. And the Spirit of God was hovering over the face of the waters" (Gen. 1:2).

Formless and void. Covered in darkness. This planet, now so full of activity, at one point was indistinguishable from Pluto or Mars. Such places are awe inspiring, yes, but no breath of life exists on them.

"Without form and void" is another way of saying chaotic and orderless. Before God moved his hand in creation, there was nothing but unformed, chaotic potential. Sounds much like the work environments many of us find ourselves in every day. And that's to be expected: after all, they are waiting for us to partner with the Almighty to create something good.

So here at the beginning of creation, we find the definition of good work: good work creates something good where nothing good once existed.

That's it. It sounds simple, but good work requires an entirely different approach from other work. You can't achieve good work just by applying more elbow grease. To do good work, you must participate in the good work God already has a mind to do. You must move from chaos to creative order. And that takes prayerful observation.

The Spirit of God is always hovering over something: formless and empty situations, people, and projects. Each one of them needs the goodness of God to supernaturally transform its current state. That's next-level kind of work, and you can never reach it so long as you're going solo. Until you partner with the Almighty, all you can offer is mere excellence or hard work.

Situations that need godly goodness are all around you. These are the places where God's great task of bringing relief to the oppressed is happening. These needs exist everywhere on your jobsite as well. Start looking for them intently, with an eye toward involving yourself in them. Look for gaps in goodness around you, and begin to step into them, asking God to do his works through you. When you have brought compassion, comfort, encouragement, or hope to someone who was suffering, you can know for certain that your work looks like Christ's work.

Start there. Invade the void. Form the formless. Work with the Spirit of God. This is the practical part of God's promise to work all things *toward* the good (see Rom. 8:28). You may not be creating a new heaven and earth, but you can certainly participate in the new reality of the kingdom.

But you do still have to tend to customers and lunch rushes and purchase orders. And that means you'll have to get practical about good work. You'll need to get off your knees in prayer and actually partner with the presence of God. You'll need to start calming the chaos, which is something you're perfectly capable of doing with God's help.

So how do you do this? All *good* work shares three traits. Good work is always intentional, relational, and timely. This is how faith and actions can work together.

INTENTIONAL WORK

We'll start with intentionality. Creation was, after all, on purpose. Your work must be the same.

In original creation, there was potential for beauty and life, but none yet existed. Before the good was formed, there was nothing but chaos. Water and wind. The first thing God did was lay a purposeful foundation. He brought purpose to something that lacked life. So intentional work, from a spiritual perspective, is eliminating chaos and bringing purpose to everything that is being done.

In this way, we're not *just* making sure everything we do supports coworkers in a loving way—we're also providing peace through clarity. We make prayerful, conscious decisions to eliminate the angsty, chaotic, restless work that the world is always acting out. "Peace. Be still" is a way of working. A mode of operation.

To this end, intentional work is also restful work. God may have put in a full day's work, but he did so from a place of rest. He hovered—he didn't heave. When we operate from the peace of God, our work carries with it a sense of rest.

If we work like this, we can be confident that whatever we do will bless others and eliminate suffering. Why? Because we're operating without anxiety. There's nothing to get worked up about. There is no formless, void anxiety in our hearts to sway our thinking.

RELATIONAL WORK

Next, we have relational work. Everything the Lord does is relational.

In creation we can observe a masterful order of operations. Everywhere around us, the earth's systems support and coexist with one another. The sun heats the ocean, causing the rain to nourish the ground. The ground bears fruit that feeds the animals, which, in turn, support you and your family. All this happens with beautiful precision.

Our work should look the same: it should support those around us. Look for how your work could accomplish the greater good. Ask yourself, "How can this work contribute to the mission of Christ on the earth?"

Everything you do should live beyond itself in this way. The challenge for you is not simply to finish the task at hand but also to seek how any task can give glory to God well beyond completion of the task itself.

This could be the way you organize your tasks, how you leave a work area for the next person, or simply the way you communicate to others with kindness. Ultimately, it is about being aware of your work environment. Your work should support the ongoing efforts of those around you, whether they're customers, coworkers, or clients. Remember how Solomon's work caused the queen to wonder at the wisdom and goodness of God (see 1 Kings 10:1–9).

TIMELY WORK

Timeliness has two parts: it is not rushed, and it is not late.

Good work takes time. And it *should* take time. God could have fit his entire creation process into a day or a millisecond, no doubt, but he did not. He gave each day its own effort and each new project the time it deserved. If he hadn't, the work might not have been as good as we experience it. This has application for us too. Scripture reminds us, "The plans of the diligent lead to profit as surely as haste leads to poverty" (Prov. 21:5 NIV).

The proverb isn't teaching that working slowly is always great or that working with haste is always bad. It's saying that the man who takes the time to think about what he's going to do stands a much better chance of succeeding than the man who decides to do some big project and then runs off willy-nilly to try to get it done.

Nor are we dealing with dueling personalities, like some sort of Mary and Martha situation (see Luke 10:38–42). Which is where wisdom comes into play.

The opposite of hurried work is not slow or methodical toil. Nor is it about being a "be-er" versus a "doer." The Christian man seeks the Lord before beginning new work so he can understand the pitfalls and potential outcomes of which he needs to be aware. He equips himself with wisdom as he plans.

Hard and quick work without diligent planning is wasted and will likely result in exhaustion, burnout, and, if it becomes a habit, a reputation for less-than-excellent work. Do yourself a favor: learn to plan well. Measure twice; cut once.

If you think planning isn't your job, think again. Whom else might the responsibility belong to? It's not the job of your manager, your coworker, or your wife to figure out how you can be more timely or efficient. It's *your* responsibility. If they help you, that's fine, but ultimately, you're the owner of your work. So find a balance that includes excellence and efficiency. If you're an entrepreneur or own your own business, you may even need to stop and define a new habit of planning that will be appropriate for the type of work you do.

This kind of planning makes some men nervous. Not to worry. Timeliness is an opportunity to show how you excel at your vocation. The more you surround your process with the supernatural wisdom of timekeeping, the more evident it will be that you do good work.

Ask the Lord for understanding about how you can best organize your time. It's a simple but powerful way to serve those around you.

WHAT ABOUT YOUR WORK?

Is the work you do *good*?

If we're honest, we have to say that good work can be done only in partnership with the Holy Spirit. He is the one who enables us to live with a good, new nature. So it stands to reason that your work, which is an extension of you, will be enabled in the same way. When you prayerfully pursue his perspective, you produce good work. It's an outcome of relationship.

Without his guidance, your work ethic will turn into a flesh-driven endeavor. Indeed, we can justify a lot of apathy, bad attitudes, and pride if we hide behind the idea of working hard. Hiding behind this idea can also open us to a mentality of *I work hard, so I have license to do what I want*. Not a place you want to be.

Who cares if you worked harder than the next guy? Who cares if you go home tired? What are you leaving on the field when you leave anyway? If your work isn't *good*, then what you have earned is a nice little trophy for your self-effort and pride. Plain and simple.

Work ethic is a muscle. But for the Christian man, it is not strengthened by labor alone. A Christ-honoring work ethic is the outcome of sanctification. It is the product of godly surrender of every thought, emotion, and situation during the day.

Let a new kind of work ethic grow in your life—one rooted in faith and not simply function. Let it be evidence of the Almighty. If only because you want Christ to grow in your life as well.

The Lord knows, though, that it is much harder for us to produce good, faith-filled work than it was for him to create the cosmos. By Wednesday our spirits may not even be hovering. They could be drowning in a sea of paperwork, work orders, or other less-than-ideal things to do. This tired toil can actually be worse for a Christian than it would be for an unsaved man, if the believer feels that he must "act Christian." That can add pressure to always play the part of a good guy. And anytime a man feels pressure to behave in a certain way, it can set him up for fear that he won't succeed.

Brother, you *will* grow weary in doing good works if you believe they are a means to an end. But you can persevere in them if you see they are an end in and of themselves. We don't work to impress God or impress others. But the work we do should evidence godly wisdom, virtue, and creative problem-solving. This is true of Christ's work. This is true of creation. And this is true of what you create as well.

You do not need to "pay it forward" or live out some kind of Hallmark-card holiness in order for your work to look like Christ's. Good work is all we aim for. You live out your calling by action. Your actions, the practical things you do—when they are full of the wisdom of God, full of the Holy Spirit, and full of your relationship with Jesus—are the actions of a called man. They're all you need to aim for.

Trust me—if you don't act in this way, you will get exhausted or depressed or both. You will be frustrated when others don't work as hard as you are working. You will start to evaluate work using an earthly-minded scale. You will begin seeing things solely based on performance and practicality rather than goodness and kingdom.

Paul described his experience with the early church this way: "By the grace of God I am what I am, and his grace toward me was not in vain. On the contrary, I worked harder than any of them, though it was not I, but the grace of God that is with me" (1 Cor. 15:10). The Apostle could have proved a point based on his effort alone, but he knew it was better to let the grace of God operate through him in the work of church planting he was called to do.

You are what you are, just as Paul was who he was. You are a man saved, sanctified, and repurposed in new life. The blanket of God's grace covers all of us the same. Now, you might not be in the Corinthian church, but you do have your own work in which you must struggle and remain steadfast.

We can learn from Paul's experience. Grace is not given in vain. Indeed, it encourages us to trust God to work through us. So, then, we make this great Corinthian commitment along with all the Christian men who have gone before us. Chests up. Chins high. "My beloved brothers, be steadfast, immovable, always abounding in the work of the Lord, knowing that in the Lord your labor is not in vain" (1 Cor. 15:58).

Be steadfast. Be immovable. Be as committed to God in your actions as God has been committed to you. Abound in good work— not because you have to work hard but because it's an honor to live out your calling. Make it a pledge, and your hope will be firm. Do this, and you will always experience abundance. Remind yourself of this every day. No labor, when given to the Lord, is in vain. It accomplishes its purpose.

We have God as our example in this also. Consider the cross.

"It is finished," Christ said (John 19:30). How different life would be if he'd simply said, "I worked hard!" What pitiable men we'd be. Thank God that he finishes what he starts. In both his creative work and the work of his Spirit.

So here we also become like Christ in the way we approach our challenges within the working day. We face them by mindfully abiding in Christ the entire day and seeking the will of the Father. This is the foundation of good work.

In light of all this, how do we do our jobs, whatever they may be, as unto the Lord?

It's a loaded question. We know that work must take on a different meaning for the Christian. The old man is gone. So are all his earthly work habits.

But now you have a new habitation. A new home for your heart. Because of this, the new man's work is more about godliness than grit.

You see, with his grace comes the power to transform your work *gracefully*. If you do not submit yourself to this daily given grace, then you will impose a flesh-driven work cycle on yourself. Not to mention the very people to whom you are called to minister. Persistence is valuable.

But there is no substitute for godly vision.

GOOD AND GODLY VISION

In Proverbs, Solomon reminded us to check our hearts for vision (see 29:18). This is wonderful wisdom because it reminds us that there is a blessing for not relying on our strength alone to push through the day. True, there is a certain pride we feel in powering through and having the mind-set of *When the going gets tough, the tough get going.* It feels good. It feels right.

Unchecked, it is a deeply rooted arrogance.

So check yourself. Seek first the kingdom (see Matt. 6:33). Take your best to the Lord in the work you do—but only from a position of grace and gratitude. Do not follow in the way of Cain, taking work that, while honest in the flesh, is not the good firstfruits of your heart (see Gen. 4:3–7). You don't need to earn the favor of your Father. There is no spiritual paycheck to be earned from God. No heavenly time card to be punched. Only recognize that this life and the work within it are a gift. So we treat our work lives as if they're gifts we can give back to God.

A great deception that some Christian men embrace is the idea that simply punching their time cards means that their work is dedicated to the Lord. But that couldn't be further from the truth. You can go your entire life putting time into your work life and never get around to the reason the Almighty provided you the job to begin with: *good* work.

Remember, the world's workers seek what they think work can give them. All the while, your heavenly Father has already given you something that work hours cannot earn. God wants to free you from doing your job for the sole purpose of providing for your family.

Scripture says the Lord owns "the cattle on a thousand hills" (Ps. 50:10). That means that he, being a good father, knows how to provide for you. So let him.

Ultimately, he is the provider for you and your family. He wants you to keep this in the forefront of your mind so that you are focused on the right things. He wants you working spiritually smarter, not physically harder. As with all his children, he is looking for those to whom he can entrust his heart. If your heart is completely focused on the cares of this world, you won't have energy for the cares he has for this world. Seek out his will. He'll put food on the table. He'll even trade you toil for tranquility.

In large and small moments, we are all standing before the Almighty. There is nothing hidden. We are positioned in imperfect humility toward our Creator. What a grace it is that we do not have to wait until heaven to have the tally counted. For we are counted as sons now. We are born again. We are unified in rebirth now. The only work we need to focus on is the kingdom's. If we do this, God has promised to take care of the rest.

So give yourself to him. Give yourself to him each day. Advance your career, this holy hustle of yours, through good work.

Each day brings with it a void. A formless opportunity to bring in good and light. And it waits on you. Do not hide your light. It will boldly advance into the darkness of your work environment.

Indeed, the Spirit of God within you is ready to do good work through you. Let him. Light overcomes darkness. Good work is evidence of much more than skill.

Now go create something good where nothing good has existed.

Daily Prayer

Father, by your Spirit, make me steadfast. Make me immovable. May the work of my hands be your work.

Remind me, whenever I feel weary, that laboring with you is never in vain. Create in me a desire to do good work. Not simply excellent or well meaning.

Help me, as well, to see where I've set my standards for a job well done a little too low. I want the outcome of my work to demonstrate your goodness.

Thank you also for doing good work in me. I'm amazed at your work in my life. Help me walk in humility because of that reality.

I do not want hard work to be a god I serve. I do not want to commit sweat idolatry.

Empower me, simply, to do all my work as unto you, whatever that may look like today.

In Christ, amen.

Chapter 11

THE RIVER AND THE RESURRECTION

He who believes in Me, as the Scripture said, "From his innermost being will flow rivers of living water."

—John 7:38 NASB

One summer I took a canoe down the Brazos River with some friends. The river looked nearly as wide as it was long, winding some 1,280 miles through the High Plains and Blackland Prairie. In Texas it is the longest body of water around, which meant the landscapes it took us through were prime for exploration.

The river gave us options. Sometimes we'd coast past foreboding banks that looked like trouble. Other times we would take the trouble on ourselves and jump from rocky ledges with no care for what the water held for us. It was all a thrill. And there was no real worry that we wouldn't reach our destination. The river's current was always there to move us forward.

Throughout the trip the river did most of the work for us. In the center of its current, we hardly needed our paddles. The water guided us down its winding path—and we rested as it pulled us along.

In fact, it sometimes took more work to stay still. More than once, the river pulled our beached canoes away from the bank without us. The current gently drew them back into its flow. Each time, we had to splash into the water and pull them back up onto the bank if we were really intent on staying put. The current called us onward.

There is a current flowing in your own life, brother. God gave it to you for exploration and enjoyment. This current is his favor in your life, expressed through your unique giftedness at work. When you're in Christ, the canoe can hardly be stopped. You'll be forever headed toward the beautiful landscape to which God's giftedness can take you.

This is what God means your work life to be: a continuous exploration of his goodness through partnership with him. That partnership might take you through high plains of promise or far-away careers or through hidden canyons of deep effectivity. But no matter where you go, the current of his favor will carry you forward—if you let it.

In case you've never heard this before, I want to make it clear: God is going to use your gifting through his divine inspiration in your role at work. This is a partnership. The two of you working together. It is the practical part of "Thy kingdom come, Thy will be done in earth, as it is in heaven" (Matt. 6:10 KJV).

The early Christians were taught to be aware of this grace of giftedness, but we've somehow lost this awareness over the years. I want you to consider Paul's encouragement in Romans:

> Having gifts that differ according to the grace given to us, let us use them: if prophecy, in proportion to our faith; if service, in our serving; the one who teaches, in his teaching; the one who exhorts, in his exhortation; the one who contributes, in generosity; the one who leads, with zeal; the one who does acts of mercy, with cheerfulness. (12:6–8)

When we are born again, God shows grace to us through a variety of gifts. Think of it like getting part of an inheritance early or opening a present the day before Christmas. It's a little fun before the big event. God wants us to enjoy his goodness—and his power— long before we're through the pearly gates. But the gifts we receive will look different for each person.

All Christians experience this giftedness but in different ways. Notice how Paul lumped a myriad of gifts together. The gift of prophecy looks a lot different in practice from the gift of hospitality, but they're both made of the same stuff. Your fingers do one set of things, and your ears do another, but they all have the same blood flowing through them. And they all contribute to the health and effectiveness of the person.

Some Christian men think that, in order to do God's work, they must have strictly spiritual gifts, like prophecy, evangelism, or exhortation. From Romans 12, that's obviously not the case. Every gift needs the power of God, yes. A light is useless without electricity. A river doesn't rush without a current. But if you've thought you needed a certain type of giftedness before you could do the Lord's work, you can set that idea aside. God actually calls you *through* the type of giftedness he placed within you.

All categories of giftedness give you agency to do the work of the Lord here on the earth. They move you forward into the Great Commission and the call of the kingdom. As a man abides in Christ, these gifts make a path for him in ways he might not even imagine.

I have seen this principle play out time and time again in my own life. One time in particular was before an important meeting.

DIVINE INSPIRATION

Many people consider them boring, but I love a good meeting. The higher the stakes, the better. A meeting is a chance to get things done, a bit of time when we get to be accountable to progress. And this midweek meeting was more important than most.

I had been asked to consult the company and its leadership team on how both they and the company were doing. My task was to tell them how I thought they could improve.

My initial thought, when presented with the task, was *Where do I begin?* Not that they were doing anything wrong. But I had a laundry list of things I could tell them, based purely on my experience and personality. I also knew, however, that all my advice, while superficially good, was opinion driven. Working from that place has never gotten me far, spiritually speaking. It's like paddling a canoe against the current: you'll work twice as hard and get half as far.

So before I prepared my report, I prayed. "God, you know much better than I what will help this company be successful and how it can be made to look more like the kingdom. I know what I might tell them, but what answers would you give them?"

You see, my gifting is mostly in leadership and—to a lesser extent—prophecy. Those gifts are ever-present in me, but that does not mean I'm always keen to abide with the Almighty in exercising them.

Part of the way I orient myself is by choosing to first lead my own heart by bringing that gifting back before the Lord. Otherwise, I'm a rogue agent operating only on my own insight and strength.

I look at God's process of gift giving like riding a bike. When I was young, my dad gave me a brand-new bike. I couldn't have been more excited when he presented it to me. I'd always wanted a bike. I knew deep in my nine-year-old heart that bike riding was the life for me. And this one was mine to keep. But I didn't know how to ride it. My father needed to teach me. So we rode our bikes together. I learned from observation and from simply enjoying the ride alongside him.

Partnership with God happens the same way. The gifts are always ours, but they're much more fun and effective in relationship. They're meant to be shared, both with God and with others. So I do my best to ask him how I should use my gifting, and he teaches me.

This discipline echoes the earlier part of Romans 12, about how we should live in light of this giftedness:

> I appeal to you therefore, brothers, by the mercies of God, to present your bodies as a living sacrifice, holy and acceptable to God, which is your spiritual worship. Do not be conformed to this world, but be transformed by the renewal of your mind, that by testing you may discern what is the will of God, what is good and acceptable and perfect. (vv. 1–2)

As we present our bodies—the whole of who we are—as living sacrifices, our giftedness is brought into the spiritual service of worship. In fact, offering ourselves to God is a prerequisite for those gifts to be influential.

In my own life, if I do not live this way, my gifts quickly become self-oriented. Outside Christ's empowerment, the gifts will be conformed (i.e., lowered) to worldly thinking, and I'm not nearly as effective. People say I become a bit of a bulldozer when I'm in that mode, simply trying to move heavy loads with my own brute managerial style. This makes it hard to test and discern what is the good, pleasing, and perfect will of God for me within my calling.

Back to my little meeting. God did indeed place in my mind two major thoughts about how the company could change its direction and look more like the kingdom. I knew the insights were special, and I knew I never would've landed on this information myself. However, I also perceived that God had left it to me to organize the implementation of the solution.

Needless to say, the effect it had on those I presented it to was immense.

The company's upper management was stunned and excited, and they immediately saw the benefit of what I was proposing—perhaps even more than I did. What was supposed to be a one-hour meeting turned into nearly two. Not only that, but I was also asked to advise on a myriad of other issues the company had behind the scenes.

I felt a little like Joseph interpreting Pharaoh's dream. It was pretty amazing. God was working through my gifting, through divine inspiration, and it was having a real-world effect on those around me.

That's an important point: at a job, revelation from God is always practical. You'll be able to put a wrench to it in some way.

The CEO came to my office soon after the meeting, sat down, and stared at the wall with a kind of happy blank stare. Not because of me, of course, but because of what God had done during the meeting. He knew there was real value in what we had talked about. The best part of it was that this opened the door for me to reveal how I'd come to those insights. And now I had both the gift and the testimony for which to give glory to God.

This is what abiding in Christ looks like on the job. This is what it looks like for God to move through a person's gifting to bring glory to himself in a job setting. The details will look different for you because you have a different gifting. But as you abide in Christ at work, the call on your life will have an outlet to manifest itself.

This is what you're aiming for. This is what makes you ready to get out of bed in the morning. But without this abiding lifestyle, you will revert to a more flesh-driven approach to work. You'll end up doing things in your own strength. That's not to say you won't get anything done, but kingdom work will be something you stumble into instead of consistently succeed at.

Jesus warned us of this: "I am the vine; you are the branches. Whoever abides in me and I in him, he it is that bears much fruit, for apart from me you can do nothing" (John 15:5).

As in all aspects of the Christian life, there is not much we can do with our giftedness at work if we don't remain in Christ. The "sap" of the Savior is what allows us to bear fruit. He is what gives ongoing life to our calling.

REAL TESTIMONY

Most people who don't know the Lord try to live moral lives. They don't understand how the Christian life is any different. And when morality is all we offer them at work, they think they already have that. If we aren't also demonstrating how God can influence the practical stuff during the day, we lose out on demonstrating the power of the gospel.

I saw this in a profound way during a consulting gig I sat in on. I was newly hired at a company, and a client of ours wanted to break their contract. They were paying us a large amount to help them grow their business, and they were seeing no return. Anyone, Christian or not, would have an issue with this, don't you think?

I drove to their office with our owner, who wanted to personally try to save the account. But before going in, he decided to pray. He prayed that our unsaved team members would come to know Jesus by how he, the owner, handled himself. He also prayed that the client would have mercy on us and that we would find favor with them during the meeting. The prayer was as heartfelt as any I've ever heard.

When he finished praying, he looked at me and said, "You know what? I'm going to take a different approach. I'm just going to witness to these guys and trust that God will work out the rest."

A bold move. One that on the surface appeared to take a lot of faith. I was new on the team, so I just nodded and prayed it would work.

We went into the meeting, and the owner stood up in front of our client's leadership team. For the next forty-five minutes, he proclaimed to them personal stories of faith, told how he was involved in church, and then continued to talk about his ministry outside work. He shared his personal testimony with all the conviction you might expect from a mission trip report. When he finished preaching, he opened the floor for questions.

"Thank you for sharing that moving story," someone from the C-suite said. "But how are you going to help us close more leads with our call center strategy?"

Sadly, he wasn't prepared for the only question they desperately needed an answer to. After all, they were trusting us with a lot of money. A few days later, we lost the account. On top of that, our coworkers who didn't know the Lord remained unconvinced.

It was tragic if only because it was such a lost opportunity to demonstrate how loving God is and how much he cares for the things that burden us. Not through preaching but through the Spirit of God working through spiritual gifts … at work.

If someone with, say, the gift of hospitality and the skill for sales had used those gifts for God, the spiritual impact (not to mention the workplace testimony) would have been enough to reveal God to them.

It is safe to say that God gave us the client and we simply failed to steward them well. The testimony that could've borne fruit in the lives of those leaders was ultimately lost because we had misplaced our priorities. We did not operate from a place of giftedness, and the outcome was, sadly, rather obvious.

That doesn't mean the man should never have shared his faith. Had the opportunity presented itself naturally, he absolutely should have.

But an outsider could conclude that God was apparently not that influential because his power didn't pour over into the work we did as Christians.

I've seen this happen at the individual level as well. I once knew a woman who worked at a local bistro with a few of my unsaved friends. She was on fire for God and wanted everyone to know it. On the job she told stories of her mission trips, how she had seen new eyeballs appear in the eye sockets of the blind and had seen those in spiritual bondage become free. She even mentioned how she knew Jack Hayford, a popular minister and author, and would tell about the spiritual advice he'd given her at times.

Her coworkers were not impressed. It was not that the stories were so bad, per se, but that she constantly slowed the team down with them. They were all trying to keep drive-through traffic moving and make sure people received their coffee quickly.

She had no influence in their lives because her life failed to demonstrate practical love and leadership on the job. I have no doubt that she loved Jesus very much. But I can't help but wonder what would've happened if she had been focused on how she might support her team in a way only the love of Jesus could through her gifting. It was a missed opportunity. And sadly, she was let go after only a few months.

The world can measure only what it knows. If you've been hired to do a job and you don't do it, maybe because you'd rather talk about Jesus, then you'll be fired. That's not to say we shouldn't demonstrate the goodness of God or tell others about Jesus. But if those around us don't see the God-life influencing and *contributing to* our day-to-day work, it will leave them scratching their heads, wondering what supposedly makes this whole Jesus thing so great.

So how *do* we use our spiritual gifts on the job? How can we get practical about letting our calling flow through our career? Remember the invitation given to us clearly in James: "If you need wisdom, ask our generous God, and he will give it to you. He will not rebuke you for asking" (1:5 NLT).

God has a completely different perspective about our work than we do. But we normally don't ask him. Or we bring him into the situation only when we feel anxious or are trying to prove to someone that he is who he says he is. This isn't really the abiding that Scripture encourages us to do (see John 15:4).

The Almighty knows much better than you do how to demonstrate Christ to others. There is no doubt that our words and what we say about Jesus are important. But equally important are our actions and how we use our giftedness through the work we do during the day.

This is good news. God does not give you a bike and then not teach you how to ride. He is generous not only in his distribution of gifts but also in the wisdom about how to use them.

How can you abide in Christ at work? How do you stay in the vine while on the job? There are two ways:

> 1. Ask God to reveal the approach he would like you to use at work. How would he like you to *be* when you're on the clock?
> 2. Ask God what he thinks about a specific task. How does he see you and this work situation in light of what he's called you to do and the way

he wants you to love other people with your own
unique giftedness?

When you ask these two questions, you are doing the practical, nuts-and-bolts work of abiding. Simply turning your mind to
inquire of God during your day is building a discipline of remaining
in Christ. You can apply this abiding process to whatever spiritual
gift you have. The reason it works so well is that it is relational. When
you involve God in this specific way, you choose to be vine oriented
instead of vocation oriented.

When you ask God how he'd like you to approach work, you
may not hear the audible voice of God. Then again, you might. But
there is a much better way to see evidence that the work you're doing
is connected to the kingdom: the fruit you bear.

YOU WILL KNOW THEM BY THEIR FRUIT

Fruit in the Christian's life is the evidence both that he is in Christ
and that he is doing the work of the kingdom.

Fruit is the outcome of abiding, of growth, and of communion
with Christ. It is what we bear by being born again.

And it is much, much more than simply virtue. This is important to know because the Enemy or our insecurity can lead us to fake
the virtues of the Christian life rather than abiding in them. The
distinction is subtle, but the difference is profound—especially as it

pertains to the unique gifts God has given each of us to use within our calling.

"The fruit of the Spirit is love, joy, peace, forbearance, kindness, goodness, faithfulness, gentleness and self-control. Against such things there is no law" (Gal. 5:22–23 NIV).

Pay attention to this statement: "Against such things there is no law." The author gave it to us for a reason. Very often, when work gets hard or we find ourselves in a situation where we need to witness to our faith, we find ourselves in need of the virtues that Galatians outlines.

You'll notice, however, that it does not tell us to *be* loving, joyful, peaceful, forbearing, kind, good-natured, faithful, gentle, or self-controlled. And for good reason. Those aren't our fruit—they are the Spirit's fruit. We can't manifest them by trying hard. They flow through us from Christ, or they don't, regardless of what we work hard to manifest. But often, when we don't know what to do, how to act, or how to show Christ to those around us, we try to put on those virtues in the hope that we'll seem more Christlike to those hurting people.

This doesn't work. And when we act this way, even if we're well meaning, the very thing that was meant to be evidence of our freedom in Christ becomes a law of bondage for us. Acting this way will get us into trouble, and people can see right through it. The world is also trying to be these things (loving, patient, and the rest), and without Christ creating those things in us, we'll see about the same success as they do.

What we want, then, is to manifest this fruit of the Spirit at work without becoming pharisaical. This happens only by abiding in Christ, using our unique gifting, through divine inspiration, on the jobsite (and off).

When we abide in Christ at work, we are well on our way to living every day in the midst of the work we've been called to do. The fruit of the Spirit will manifest itself on its own. When you are abiding in Christ, you can't help but be peaceful. Can't help but be joyful. And loving and kind and self-controlled and the rest.

And God will show you how to apply that fruit to your work. You will know how to do the job when others may not. You'll have a plan come to your mind when there had been only obstacles. You'll be a better leader than everyone in the room because you have insight that only God could have given you.

This is how your coworkers come to know the Lord and how they begin to trust that you aren't simply doing this Christ-walk in your own strength. The power of God will be undeniable. Evidence of the goodness of God will abound everywhere because you're operating in it regularly.

Against such testimony of divinely inspired work, so full of both the wisdom and the way of God, there is no law. There is no objection. There is no condemnation. There is no judgment. Your work will be a powerful testimony to the nature of God.

Dedicate your hands as tools that are set apart for a kingdom cause. When given a task you don't enjoy, abide in Christ. When your boss is being unfair, ask God how he wants you to respond.

When it's hard to see purpose in what you're doing, partner with the Lord and let him transform your job.

Be a conduit. A lightning rod. Expect to be hit with the lightning of heaven during a storm. Whatever you reach for will move through you and into others.

THE TORCH OF TESTIMONY

You cannot separate the nail and cross from Christ's hand between them. Neither can you separate your strength from Christ's sacrifice. Yes, many men died on crosses. All to death—only one to resurrection. Many men work their entire lives. Some to death—others to life. But the man bound by the blood of Christ can bear resurrected results.

You can do the same type of work as other men, be neck and neck with them in talent, yet have a completely different outcome in your work. Because of the vine. Because of the blood. Because of the new life in your veins. Stand up, man—you're resurrected. In this new life, take part in the race that Paul loved so well:

> As for you, always be sober-minded, endure suffering, do the work of an evangelist, fulfill your ministry.
>
> For I am already being poured out as a drink offering, and the time of my departure has come. I have fought the good fight, I have finished the race,

I have kept the faith. Henceforth there is laid up for
me the crown of righteousness, which the Lord, the
righteous judge, will award to me on that day, and
not only to me but also to all who have loved his
appearing. (2 Tim. 4:5–8)

In our jobs we can crave the appearing of Christ. And the
hope set before us, the crown of righteousness, waits for those who
continue well. What assurance this is for us. It is a promise for the
paralyzed. It is water for the weary runner. You have no idea how
much good God has in mind for you. How untapped his potential
within you is. He's given you himself. A lifelong running partner. As
we abide in Christ, he leads us onward.

Run, brother. Run. Run as far as you think the Father is capable
of taking you. He makes mountains low. He makes valleys high.
Every conceivable roadblock crumbles at the name of Jesus. His
truth is terraformed around you. Reality responds to his righteousness within you. He knows the road ahead. All you need to do is take
the next step.

So have you seen? Or have you heard? Do you have any trophies
of his victory close at hand? Mile markers that point the way forward? Fruit that remains?

Testimony is a torch. It pushes the darkness of doubt or discour-
agement away. You need this testimony to stay encouraged at work
and in your calling. Yes, it lives within you already. But we're not
talking about a Sunday school story or your great-grandma's mis-
sionary tales. These won't do at all. You need regular reminders that

the Lord is working with you already. That is, if you want to see your surroundings correctly.

If you don't see correctly, you'll get lost. You will be left with distant hills—other people's stories and spiritual successes—to guide you. It's true that other people's testimonies can be inspiring. They can be innovative as well.

However, they do not help much in the moment if you don't have any of your own. You regularly need new stories of you and the Father working together so you can stay encouraged during the day. These stories will be your torches. You need them to remind yourself that great distances have, in fact, been covered—that you're still in the game.

If you don't have these footnotes of faith, then your godly ambition will inevitably be choked out when work worry comes your way. In fact, this is how apathy at work is born. When you are tied down to tasks and not to a testimony, a type of spiritual rigor mortis sets in. The soul becomes set in its ways. You start desiring escape more than election. Entertainment more than eternity.

DREAM LIKE JESUS

There is only one way to break this. You will need to dream again.

No, not la-la land. Not a trance. Not even a "desk dream" at three in the afternoon. What you need instead is a picture of what could be. You need a glimpse of the unlit reality in front of you.

God gives us a new name to call him when we feel as if testimony is lacking in our lives: Yahweh Shammah, which literally means "the Lord is there." Originally it was the name given to the millennial city described in the book of Ezekiel (see 48:35).

This unique name of God is meant to set our hearts and hope on a different future. It is the foundation of his promise to complete the good work he started in us (see Phil. 1:6). To bring us to our final resting place. To help us cross the finish line on streets of gold.

For your future, your work, and your calling to be clearer than you can currently imagine, he must be there in them. Perhaps that is no surprise. But how does this knowledge manifest itself in your life?

You alone must cultivate a deep, deep ache for the Lord to be present in your work. A desire above all others. Before you put the keys in the truck, before the radio turns on, and before you call the boss man about the day, there needs to rest in you a simple, fervent prayer. Consider something like this:

Yahweh Shammah, come.
Dream Maker, come.
Inhabit my heart so we dream of the same future.
Let my left foot be forward,
the right on a firm foundation.
Be the light on my path,
The sage of my story.

When you pray like this, you will find that all worry, all angst, and all signs that the race is lost are nothing more than highway noise. You can ignore it because your face is set like flint toward the finish line. The hope of glory. The expectancy that one day you will get to see Jesus face to face. That you might hear the words "Well done, good and faithful servant" (Matt. 25:23).

As you already know, nothing can separate you from the life God has for you in Christ. Nothing can break you free from this promise. Not death or life or angels or demons or the present or the future or any powers or height or depth—or anything else in all creation—will be able to put space between you and the Almighty's love (see Rom. 8:38–39). Not even deadlines, angry customers, or poor leadership—though they would like to think they could try.

No, sir. The wind is at your back. A great cloud of witnesses—a mighty band of brothers who can each testify to a lifetime of fulfilling, faith-filled work—are cheering you on.

This is the flag and freedom of a man who wants to run in redemption's race. When you present yourself to God as you are, approved and unashamed, you gain momentum, like a marathoner running downhill. Your stride gets longer. You cover ground faster. Heaven is nearly in sight.

There is no work that Jesus cannot redeem. No career that cannot be a conduit for calling. This is the business he's in. Awaken to it.

Daily Prayer

Great and holy Father. Lead me to the cross. Lead me to the work of your Son's hands. Fill my heart with the reality and wonder of that work.

I open my heart to partnership with you in telling others of that work. In that, show me how the gifting you gave me can be part of the kingdom work you've called me to do. I want to work with you. Teach me your ways. Show me your thoughts. May I abide in you fully today.

My desire is to be full of you, full of your stories, full of the testimony of the cross. Let your light shine through me, through my work, so that others may come to know you as I have.

I love you.

In Christ, amen.

Dig deeper on your own or with a group.

Visit **awakencalling.com** for free bonus materials including:

- Questions to help facilitate group discussions
- Videos for each chapter
- Updates from Pierce
- And more

Awaken your calling, online.
Visit **awakencalling.com**